ton

Crazy Horse

CRAZY HORSE

Emlyn Hughes

Arthur Barker Limited   London
A subsidiary of Weidenfeld (Publishers) Limited

I would like to express my thanks to James Mossop, without whose help this book would never have been written.

Emlyn Hughes OBE

Contents

Illustrations

To the memory of my late father,
the greatest man who ever lived.
If only he could have lived to see Emlyn junior . . .

Prologue

RIDING THROUGH THE STREETS OF LIVERPOOL ON the Wolverhampton Wanderers' team bus and every face outside is laughing. 'All the best, Emlyn lad,' they are saying. And they are holding up two fingers on one hand, while forefinger and thumb are curled into a zero on the other.

'All the best, lad, but you'll get done 2–0' ... only a Scouser could divide his loyalties in that way.

Up at the front of the bus sits Bill Shankly, and for the first time in his life he's not wearing a red shirt or red tie on match-day. It must be the only time he has ever arrived at Anfield in the away team's company. After all, he is Mr Liverpool, the architect of the progress that has made LFC the most famous, feared and respected initials in football.

It is a very special day indeed; my first return to Liverpool as captain of Wolves. After thirteen years I feel as though I'm going home. I want to leap off the bus to shake every hand, and then I remember: my job is to get two points for Wolves and leave the friendships until afterwards.

But it was difficult because I was walking into a welcome so rich and warm that a feeling I'd never known before went coursing through my body. I never believed that guff about the hairs on the back of your head rising, but that's what happened when I led my Wolves out on to the Liverpool pitch.

The whole day was something of a footballing romance. I knew that returning to Anfield would be an emotional occasion and I tried to bury the thought. But there was no escape. Even in training the week before, I realized that the lads felt I was heading for a unique experience. Even the bus driver, as we left Molineux on the Friday evening for the drive to Liverpool, caught the fever. 'This is your big one,' he said, and I knew that everyone was with me. Every time I reminded myself that it was just another game an inner voice said, 'You must be joking!'

We arrived at the Holiday Inn in Liverpool and I seemed to know every face on the staff. It had been the scene of countless team meetings with Liverpool and the venue for several dinners, especially those connected with my own testimonial year. I bought some friends a drink and was in my room by 9.30 pm. The telephone never stopped ringing. My room-mate, Derek Parkin, must have been fed up. Every call carried a good-luck message, qualified by the fact that they were all Liverpool supporters!

The following morning they started again and, of

course, there was the inevitable rasping bark of Bill Shankly on the end of one of them.

He was there in the foyer when we came down for our light lunch. Joining us at the table, he looked at the young faces of some of the Wolves players he had never met and just said, 'Jesus Christ, boys, isn't it grand to be alive!'

They laughed. But I knew what he meant. He was saying that it was grand to be a young and fit footballer, sitting in the best hotel in Liverpool, preparing to go out and play a game you enjoyed, and being paid for it as well. The message may have been lost on one or two of them, but it registered immediately with me.

Off we went to the ground and suddenly I knew how visiting teams must have felt for a dozen years as they approached Anfield. The streets are alive with confident men. They know their team is the best. They laugh and sing and portray a humour not to be found elsewhere. But beneath all the laughter and fun there is a core of steel and the visitor knows that for ninety minutes the welcome mat is withdrawn.

In the cramped Anfield car-park people pressed against the side of the bus and there was a cheer as I got out and pushed my way through and found myself in the corridor leading to the dressing-rooms. The noise died away and I turned left into the visitors' dressing-room.

That was a peculiar feeling. For nearly thirteen years I had been turning right. I went along to the players' lounge where the guests and directors and everyone else I met pumped my hand and wished me luck. My old friend Bob Moss, who was such a fervent Liverpudlian that he would stand at Anfield just to watch the grass grow, was wearing Wolves' colours. He had been given seats in the directors' box by Liverpool secretary Peter Robinson and warned me that if I saw a disturbance in the box I was to take notice. It would be him being ejected for anti-Liverpool, pro-Hughes activities.

I read some telegrams and it was soon time to lead out the team. The TV people asked me to pause at the top of the stairs, walk slowly down and then run out on to the pitch in the normal way.

There was nothing normal about my entry into the arena that day. Almost fifty thousand people just stood and cheered me. It was an incredibly moving experience. It was their way of saying thank you for the service I had given them as a Liverpool player. I would have been disappointed had there been no reception, but this was something beyond my wildest dreams.

I went to toss up with Phil Thompson, the lad who took over from me as Liverpool's skipper. Phil knew I always called heads. A fierce sun was burning in over the famous Spion Kop roof and I desperately wanted that sun to be shining in Ray Clemence's eyes during the first half. I called 'heads', it came down tails and the smile that spread across Phil Thompson's face said everything. 'Bad luck, Emma,' he said, and I suspect he didn't mean a word of it. He knew exactly what I was after. I like to think Phil learned a few things from me during our seasons together at Liverpool.

With the niceties over it was down to business, and we were in serious trouble from the fourth minute. Unfortunately I was not entirely blameless as Liverpool scored the goal no visiting team can afford to give them.

We had a free kick on the half-way line. I took it, but never really put enough height on the ball and it was cleared straight back at us. The ball was played wide to Ray Kennedy who had twenty yards spare on his own to run at the edge of our penalty area. I knew from all the years of playing with him that he would curl one in, left peg, towards the near post. He did exactly that but I had read his intentions too early and as the ball flew in at my feet I could get no power into the attempted clearance and the ball shot away to Kenny Dalglish. There is normally only one out-come when that happens and, sure enough, he just took it on and lashed it in.

It was a blow, but we had our moments on the field. I shared a few laughs with Terry McDermott, who is a very good friend and who has always been terrific fun on Eng-land and club trips. Terry likes to make long runs from the deep and I often found myself running with him. I chided him that he was getting offside and it was good to have a chuckle together even in the height of battle.

Kenny Dalglish could be a fox, too. In the second half Ray Clemence sent a long clearance ballooning downfield. David Johnson had gone wide and Kenny was backing on to me. As he realized he wouldn't get the ball, Kenny shouted, 'Go on Johnno! Go on Johnno!' I knew that David was twenty-five yards away so I just stood off, collected the ball and played it wide to Derek Parkin.

Then I said to Kenny, 'Hey, come on, I've been in this game a long time, you know!' He took the point.

We lost 3–0, but the day was full of glorious memories. The reception from the Kop at half-time was something else. What made it extra-special was the fact that during my career at Anfield I had always kept the sup-porters at arm's length. I preferred not to get too involved, unlike Joey Jones who had the Kop tattooed on his fore-arms and before matches used to shake his fists at them, urging them to get right behind the team.

I always felt that the closer a player got to the crowd, the more they would hurt him when the end came.

The crowd at Anfield used to chant and sing every player's name before matches and they had a special chorus for me, based on the old Manfred Mann hit 'The Mighty Quinn'. They used to sing of me:

> *Come on without, come on within,*
> *You've not seen nothing*
> *Like the Mighty Emlyn.*

It used to boom out from the Kop, but I never acknowledged them because I thought that as soon as I was at the end of the road they would stop the chanting and that would bite hard.

Before the start of the second half of my return with Wolves they started the chant again and I turned round and gave them the signal. The volume doubled because they realized that, at last, I was responding. I suspect they always knew that I regarded them as the best supporters in the world.

There were other memories. Up in the stands were my wife Barbara and our children Emma (who was six and a half at the time) and Emlyn (who was three and a half). It was the first time young Emlyn had ever seen me play at Anfield and I couldn't resist looking for him in the crowd and giving him a wave.

After the match there were so many people to see and so many interviews – television, national and local radio, Press – that when I finally got to the players' lounge to see the Liverpool lads and their wives they had nearly all gone. It was an unfortunate anti-climax, until I met Bill Shankly.

True to the last he was with me. 'You could have made a game of it, son,' he said. 'You could have gone in 2–1 up at half-time.'

That was Shanks, still supporting me although I knew that in a football sense we had been wiped off the face of the earth.

The whole exercise of visiting Anfield probably did the

Wolves team a lot of good. Some people at Molineux had been slightly carried away by a string of early-season results that had carried us close to the top of the First Division. It made a lot of people realize we were still a long way from being in Liverpool's class. Manager John Barnwell, his assistant Richie Barker and I had known all along that this was the case.

The pity was that my return to Anfield had to be the occasion to prove it. But it was still a memorable milestone on the long and adventurous journey that I have been so fortunate to experience.

Back
Home

WHEREVER YOU STAND IN BARROW-IN-FURNESS
there is no escape from the sea and ships and the deeds of
men who helped to win wars. Huge cranes tower over the
waterfront. The streets are named after great vessels and
admirals: Blake, Hood, Parry, Nelson, Raleigh, Cook,
Anson, Keppel ... there is a sea battle on every corner.
Barrow folk are proud of the part they played in the days
when Britannia ruled the waves.

I was born in Blake Street. The wind whistles in from
the Irish Sea across the land where the blast furnaces of the
old iron and steel company used to hiss and snort. They
are closed now and a lot of life has gone out of the old town.

Blake Street, especially No. 94, where I was born, was

smack between two other landmarks that were to have a profound effect on my life. Only a mile or so separated the Holker Street ground of Barrow AFC and Craven Park, the home of Barrow RLFC. With a father – Fred 'Ginger' Hughes – who played rugby league for Barrow and Wales and who was, in my mind, the greatest man who ever lived, sport was always going to be a consuming influence.

The sporting life dawned gradually. When I was a youngster the family moved from Blake Street to Vale Cottage in a place called Abbots Vale, which wasn't very far from the town centre but had more open space. We had a yard and a drive and in that area some of the greatest matches of all time took place. My brothers David and Gareth and I, and a few of the local lads would split up into England and Wales. I was always on the England side. We played for hours and hours, scuffing up our shoes, developing enormous appetites and usually playing until one team had topped the 100-mark in goals.

They were unforgettable days. My brother David, who is four years older than me, often had to be coaxed into playing. He wasn't all that interested, but after leaving school he suddenly spurted ahead and went on to play rugby league for Barrow and Blackpool.

Kicking a ball about seemed to be the most natural pastime. The games themselves took on no significance at all until I was at South Newbarns Junior School where the headmaster, Joe Humphreys, was a great enthusiast. When I look back down the years now I realize the measure of debt I owe him. He fired my enthusiasm. I wanted to play every night after school, and when we did have matches I was changed and ready for action within two minutes of lessons ending.

The amount of work that people like Joe Humphreys put in often goes unnoticed. They are of great benefit to the youth of the country and that is why I like to go back for speech days and sports meetings as often as possible. I like to think I can encourage present-day youngsters.

South Newbarns were the top under-11 team in the Barrow area. We had needle matches even then. One was against St James's. They were from the Blake Street area. A hard lot. This was our own Cup final. We had a smashing little pitch with real nets and the lines marked out in white. Joe Humphreys was a linesman and as one of their lads tackled me the ball ran out of play off my foot. I raced after it, picked it up and was rushing to make the throw in when he said, 'Whose ball is it, Hughes?'

'It's ours, sir, it's ours!'

He started laughing because my enthusiasm had boiled over to the point where I was guilty of 'professional cheating' for the first time in my life.

At that stage I was years ahead of everyone in terms of sporting ability; I was strong, and could get the ball any time and run through and score. One season I scored thirty-six goals in a handful of matches and, I understand, the record still stands. I remember being kicked on the half-way line in one match. I went down rubbing my ankle in perfect imitation of a Barrow professional. Joe, who was refereeing, ran past and said, 'Get up and play, you big baby.'

Just then the ball was played straight to me. I was up, collected it and must have run through nine would-be tacklers before slotting in a goal. Then I went back to rubbing my ankle. Joe came over to me and said, 'Oh, son, I just don't know what we're going to do about you.'

He did plenty for me. From those schoolday games we extended our play. We used the pitches along Lesh Lane and our own backyard for interminable matches. Not long ago I went off to Saudi Arabia with Liverpool and the first person I met was a lad from Barrow, Geoff Lynn. He recalled one of our schoolboy feats – a corner from Geoff and there was I leaping at the far post to power home an unstoppable header. Powering home an unstoppable header? Well, that's what our memories told us!

I suppose we were lucky as kids. We always had a ball. We could not use a 'casey' because of the windows nearby and those plastic Frido balls didn't last very long. But, no matter how hard-up my mother and father may have been at times, they could always find the 3s 3d for a new one.

They were lovely days. Until a few years ago it was always my desire to move back to Barrow to live. I have a piece of land there, but the last few visits have shown me that something is lacking. It saddens me to see such a cracking little town allow its sporting interests to die. I listen to my friend Gareth Edwards talking about the passion of the Welsh valleys. I know he means it. He brought it across in his book and I always thought I would feel the same about Barrow. But I do not. The soccer team has faded into non-league. The rugby team is in the Second Division. The pitches that used to be crowded on Saturdays and Sundays and on lighter evenings are now used mainly by people walking the dog.

Perhaps the slow death of the football team has hurt me most. Barrow were my heroes. I used to follow them every single week. My younger brother Gareth and I were blue-and-white crazy.

One weekend Barrow were playing in Exeter and the eagerness to see the match became too great. We played truant, leaving Barrow on the Thursday to hitch-hike to Exeter. We slept rough, ate buns and packets of chips and saw Barrow lose 4–0. Then we set off back thumbing lifts in lorries and cars and arrived home late on Sunday.

We were not bothered about tiredness or hunger. We had

been to see Barrow. Wherever sport was involved my father always showed an understanding. He gave us a rocket when we finally trudged in through the back door, and then he provided notes to say we had been unwell and unable to attend school.

After Newbarns I attended Risedale Secondary Modern Senior School, where we had a spell of playing rugby league as well as soccer. I was picked for Barrow Boys at rugby. My father was proud. His son was playing for the town team at his own sport.

We were to play St Helens Boys up on a hill at St Aloysius School. I was stand-off half and conscious of all those bitter battles between Barrow and St Helens at senior level that had been fed to us. I was proud to be playing in the same position as Barrow's legendary Willie Horne. Willie played stand-off for Barrow and Great Britain and kicked with a round-the-corner action reminiscent of a soccer corner. We lost 47–0 and, although I was probably the smallest lad on the field, I had a feeling I'd done quite well.

As we walked off the field my father came towards me, put his arm round my shoulder and said, 'Son, you want to forget all about that game. That's the worst I have ever seen anyone play.'

I thought he was going to praise me! Anyway, that was the end of my rugby league career.

Soccer was always my first love. It had been hatched during those days at the junior school. To play at Holker Street, the actual ground where I used to watch my heroes, was a dream come true. We had to play a Schools' cup final there one day, again against the dreaded St James's.

After school I raced to the ground only to find that the other school had been there first and that their strips were hung out in the home team's dressing-room. That was a horrifying sight to my eyes. I wanted to be where my idols changed. I wanted to imagine myself as Dickie Robinson, Jackie Robertson, Tommy Cahill or Billy Gordon.

Being cast into the smaller, away dressing-room meant that I was someone from Crewe Alexandra or Workington or Gateshead, and this before the most important match of my life. With the speed and stealth of the Artful Dodger I quickly transferred their gear to the visitors' dressing-room ... and then I knew in my heart that I could go out and play like Jackie Robertson.

We were all over them. We were running here, there and everywhere, but we couldn't get the ball into the net. Two minutes from the end they broke away and in an attempt to clear one of our lads drove the ball straight at an opponent and it ballooned back over the goalkeeper's head and dropped into the goal. I walked off in tears. That match had meant so much to me. But it had been a marvellous lesson in the vagaries of sport.

Never at that stage did I realize just how much the business of winning and losing was to become a way of life.

2

Father's Way

I SOON REALIZED THAT THE SHIPYARD HOOTER that governed most people's lives in Barrow-in-Furness with its clock-on, clock-off signals was too demanding to win the respect of my father. He could make a living for himself without all that nonsense. My own reluctance to put my head in a book at school probably stemmed from his easy-going attitude. But he was a proud man and when he died five years ago I felt desolate for a long time.

My father was a local character. First and foremost he was an ex-rugby league international. He had toured with the British Rugby League Lions just after the war and always wore his blazer and badge wherever he went. He wore it so proudly and the lion seemed so big that I always felt it would have bitten off any hand that had dared reach out to touch it.

He did a bit of everything in life before starting up a tarmacadam business with a pal, a business that is now run by my brothers and is a thriving concern. The early days of his partnership are still vividly fixed in my mind. He had done his first bit of work in the Lake District with a friend when they were offered some work in Worcestershire. It was supposed to take a week. The week became a fortnight and eventually they were given a contract that would last for three months.

The family took a caravan and we camped among some gypsies just outside Tewkesbury. They were not vagabonds, they were real travelling people who had caravans smothered in silver and gold. They were wide-awake people who lived on their wits. The youngsters picked up their education along the way, but reading and writing were not important to their way of life. However, they had to go to school, and I went with them. The experience was incredible. There would be fifteen locals, ten gypsies and me in the class. In the eyes of the locals I was classed with the gypsies. The gypsies could not read or write so they classed me among the locals. Suddenly I was an amazing one-off character as far as the locals were concerned – here was an itinerant who could do all the school work that was asked of him!

We were soon back in Barrow and as we grew older my father began to steer me towards a sporting career. He was a tremendous man, a brilliant fellow. He died one night when I was playing at Manchester United. I'm glad he went that way. I didn't want to see him dragging on in a long and painful illness. I was so busy with matches and travelling at Liverpool that I saw him only twice in his sick bed. Twice was too much. Seeing the man I knew as a big, red-faced, affable character lying there weak and ailing used to tear the guts out of me.

I want my memories of him to be all good ones. And they are. Wherever I played he would be waiting for me afterwards at the gate. Even when I had played abysmally, and there were times early on when the game was a struggle, he would be there telling me I had been brilliant and that all the others were at fault for not giving me any help. He could always find an excuse for me.

At Blackpool, where he somehow managed to secure a lot of road-making contracts when I was just starting my professional career, he would knock off early and come to watch us train. Even when I was fifteen and a part-timer he would bustle into the café where such internationals as Alan Ball, Tony Waiters and Jimmy Armfield were having their cups of tea, and he would call, 'How are you, Jim?' And without waiting for a reply he would add, 'My boy is doing well, isn't he?'

He even tried his hand as a local, on-course bookmaker at the pretty Westmorland jumping track, Cartmel. The meeting always had small fields of runners and there was little class around.

It was a little family concern. My father was the bookie with the board, my mother was his clerk and Uncle Dick was away in the ring sending back the tic-tac signals relating to the prices on the other boards. Father was on his own. Not for him the silver ring where the big bookmakers and punters used to gather. Nor the enclosure where the lesser men stood. His idea of bookmaking was to have his own little stand on a hill near the start where he would take the two-bob wagers of old ladies. But that didn't stop him shouting, 'I'll take anything from a tenner to £100. Just give me your money and I'll take your bet.'

He never took more than a pound off anyone and if he

made £20 on the day he would go home happy. One day a rough-looking fellow walked up, leaned into my father and said, 'I'll have £100 the favourite.'

Father rocked back on his heels. He looked shaken. Eventually he forced out the words, 'Oh, go away please. What are you trying to do – kill me off?' He could have been £100 up, but the potential loss was too huge to contemplate.

His little pitch was known as 'Ginger's Hill'. He had been going to the same place for thirty years, continuing to visit Cartmel long after his business had started to thrive. His face was familiar to every policeman in the district (not for anything he had done, I should add) because he was a local character. He could get in anywhere. He never bothered with obtaining a licence for his bookmaking pitch and no one ever asked him to produce one. He had his own set of rules. One day there was a three-horse race and his betting board showed them at 4/6, 1/2 and even money. No punter in the world could win at those odds and yet he was taking money right and left.

As he began to get older he dropped his bookmaking but he continued to make the annual visit to Cartmel. He would have a bet and a few drinks, and the family and friends used to make it a day out.

Even when I was playing at Blackpool and Liverpool I would drive up and meet them there at the course. We were there one afternoon and father had had a few drinks and no winners. The sixth and final race was about to be run. I can see my father now, sat on the edge of the stream that runs through the course. His ginger hair, now streaked with the silver of age, was ragged and tumbling around his face which was reddened by the afternoon's drink.

He slumped forward with his hands on his knees, looking into the water for divine inspiration as he contemplated the runners in that last race.

'Son,' he said, 'We're in trouble. I don't know what we're going to do.'

He fumbled in his pocket and drew two screwed-up pound notes which he handed to me. 'Here you are, go and put two quid on the favourite.'

I took the money and he started to slide down the bank. Because of the combined forces of his drinks, the steepness of the bank and the surprise of it all he couldn't save himself and sploshed into the water.

We went after him and pulled him out. He just looked at me sadly, his day complete, and then said, 'Why did you push me in?'

He hailed originally from Llanelli in the Welsh valleys. It was mining country. There were five boys and two girls in the family and often my dad was the only one working. He never talked about it much but, occasionally, when we were wanting money for chocolate, he would just remind us that such things did not come so easily. There were times, of course, when we were stuck for things, but we never wanted the way he must have done as a youngster. I have heard tales of the family chasing through the Welsh countryside looking for a soup kitchen that might be open. But despite all the deprivations he played for the Welsh Schoolboys at rugby union and kept playing in the valleys as a young man.

He was always a bit of a wanderer, though, and he was drifting around Gloucester and Cheltenham, still playing, when a man from Barrow arrived inviting him to turn professional. He told his brothers, my uncles Emlyn, Dick and Harry, that he would sign, take the money, and then come home with it. He went up to Barrow and his first words were, 'Where is my £500?' He signed and stayed. That was it. He liked the place. He was a prop forward and later played for Workington.

For many a long hour as a kid I used to sit at his feet by the fireside listening to tales of the good old rugby days. He had played for Workington for a spell when Gus Risman, one of the most famous names in rugby league, was Workington's captain. Risman was a hard man; as tough and uncompromising as any of the later giants such as Jim Mills, Vince Karalius or Sid Hines. Workington were playing Keighley in a Cup-tie one day and everyone had been told to watch out for a bright prospect playing at centre-three-quarter for Keighley. They were not a particularly strong side and were thirty points down with the youngster showing little of his talent when suddenly he took a pass and set off. He ran wide and looked inside to send in a looping pass. His eyes were still following the ball when Gus dumped him. He lay there as though dead. He was still stone cold as they took him off on a stretcher, while Risman walked up to the referee and said, 'By the way, make sure you add on the time for that stoppage.'

A couple of years after my father's retirement it was decided to revive the Welsh rugby league international side. Most of the Welshmen in rugby league were converts from the valleys but at this particular time there were hardly enough players of Welsh birth to produce a thirteen. My dad had kept reasonably fit, but when the Welsh skipper, Gus Risman of course, came to ask him to play he declined at first.

Gus, the hard man, could also be persuasive. He told dad that experience would see him through and that there would be no need to get too involved. When they finally managed to arrive at the pre-match get-together they found that they were not only short of players but that they had no hooker and, worse still, there was no Welshman currently playing hooker anywhere in the league.

Someone remembered a fellow called Bert Day, a hooker

who had retired about four years previously. He responded to the call. He had put on weight in retirement. His legs were bandy and facing him was the best hooker in the league. My dad was Bert's prop so he heard every word of the dialogue that went on after the game had been going some time.

The Englishman was winning every ball, even at the Welsh put-in. Bert became a bit annoyed with the monotony of it all and as they packed down for another scrum he looked at the English hooker and said, 'Right lad, you've had a good time. Do that once again and I'll have you.'

Straight away the Englishman won the ball. As they got up Bert said to father, 'Right, Fred, next time you're on the opposite side of the scrum from the referee I want you to collapse it. Sure enough, just as the ball came in father dragged them all down and as he pitched forward he could see Bert's legs swinging up to catch the other fellow in the solar plexus. Every ounce of wind was driven from his body and there was just a long, agonized groan as he lay there. The pack stayed collapsed for a few minutes and as the players picked themselves up and the hooker lay there struggling for breath, Bert walked to my father and said, 'I told you I'd have him, Fred. I warned him twice.'

Such stories served to whet my appetite for sport. As soon as I started at senior school, Risedale, I showed everyone that for a youngster I had exceptional stamina. I could have played sport all day, whether it was football, rugby, cricket or athletics. My enthusiasm was boundless. Every evening I was down at the sports field, looking for a game or a chance to run. I remember going down one evening to find that the seniors, who were all four years older than me and certainly a good deal taller, were having training runs in preparation for some inter-schools cross-country championships. Among them was the star of the school, a lad called Dave Duckworth, who was brilliant at everything. They were all limbering up in their spikes for the run that would take them round the rugby and soccer fields that made up our sports grounds and those of the grammar school next door.

I went up to the master, a Mr Sewell, and said with all the confidence in the world, 'Can I have a go, sir?' He looked at me and then down at my pumps and said, 'You can, Hughes, but remember these boys are fourth-formers. They are much older than you.' I romped off with the leaders, felt quite comfortable and just kept running ahead of everyone to come home first. I think Mr Sewell thought I had cheated. But I felt so relaxed I could probably have gone round again.

The following year they put me in the school team for the races at Ulverston, a town eight miles to the north of Barrow. Schools from all over the area were taking part but the boys of Barrow Grammar School were the bees' knees. I was determined to succeed as we set off on the two $1\frac{1}{2}$-mile circuits. After a while five of us broke clear of the pack and as we came down to the winning-post for the first time round there were three of us battling together out at the front. Suddenly one of the grammar school boys spurted and opened up a gap of about ten yards. This was serious and I struggled to stay in touch but, as we came down an incline lapping some stragglers, I was baulked by one of them and stumbled and fell. The leader stole thirty or forty yards by the time I was on my feet again; even the lad in third place had caught up with me.

I set off sprinting as hard as I could go but the task was impossible and the other lad passed me on the line so that I finished third. Then I collapsed and was in such a state that they took me to hospital. I can vaguely remember seeing my parents just beyond the winning-line. My father was beaming happily because he knew I had given everything and, to him, that was just as important. Then my vision went hazy and I remembered no more. Without going into the medical terms, it seemed that in my efforts I had run all the sugar out of my blood. The result was utter exhaustion and the remedy was a diet of hot sweet tea, honey and strawberry jam. The run was typical of my determination not to be beaten although I was still younger and smaller than the other competitors.

At that point I seemed to lose everything. Until the age of thirteen I had been out on my own at sports. But for the next three or four years I seemed to stand still. Perhaps I had a spell where I was shooting up; out-growing my strength. Once the best player in the school with complete domination of the games I played in, I now found it all something of a struggle and lost a bit of interest.

But there was always my beloved Barrow. One match sticks out above all others. It was an FA Cup third round match against Wolves. They were top of the First Division but because of severe weather conditions there was a doubt that the match would be played. The pitch was in appalling condition and Billy Wright, who was Wolves' captain and England's centre-half at the time, maintains to this day that it was the worst pitch he has ever played on. During the week armies of volunteers, and I was one of them, reported to the ground with spades in an effort to make the pitch level and playable. All Friday night dozens of braziers burned on the frozen ground trying to thaw out the ice. The ground was full and the match went ahead. I stood in the paddock close to the tunnel.

Wolves were there in all their might – Wright, Ron Flowers, Eddie Stuart, Malcolm Finlayson, Peter Broadbent, Norman Deeley and so on. Barrow were drawing 2–2 at the interval and the fairy story that was being played out before my young eyes – Barrow's Jackie Robertson beating Wright to score – was shattered when Wolves went on to win 4–2.

Robertson was my own star. I used to watch everything he did and his play gave me the first inkling that a footballer needed wit and brains as well as the ability to kick the ball. Robertson was a Scottish centre-forward, but was never the type to go up and do battle with the centre-half. He was a subtle player, lying deeper than most and often drawing the centre-half out of the middle. He never got worked up into a lather and I always thought that I wanted to be a player like Jackie Robertson.

My ambition to play for Barrow was growing all the time, though I was no longer the outstanding schoolboy player of my first year at Risedale. I used to watch Barrow play and then hang around the ground to see the players afterwards. They got to know me as I walked down Holker Street alongside them. Eventually I plucked up courage and went in to ask the secretary if I could become an apprentice when I left school. They told me to join in the evening training sessions with the amateurs and the part-timers and I even had a match or two in the youth team, but I was still growing into myself. I don't blame Barrow for not taking me on, even though I subsequently made the grade. At fifteen I was showing nothing and I'm sure my father realized that when he sent me to work as a garage mechanic at a place in the aptly named Emlyn Street. The family tarmacadam business was just starting and the plan was for me to learn a trade so that if business expanded I would be equipped to look after the wagons and machinery. My heart was never in it, however. I didn't mind rising early, but I hated going to work.

My football was confined to the Barrow and District League with a team called Roose Juniors. I played on

Saturdays and Sundays and another of those men who are the body and soul of junior football, Bill Evans, was in charge. He used to live near me in Lesh Lane and through him my old enthusiasm for playing started to return. We used to meet early on match days and collect the kit and corner flags and mark out the pitch before the others came. He used to take a shilling a week from us for the kit and he always talked to us at length about how the game should be played. I often see his widow and she always says, 'Mr Evans would have been proud of you.'

He was a good man, like Joe Humphreys, who did a lot for many young people in Barrow. It's a pity there are not many of them around today. I still treasure an old school report which says, 'If this boy was as good at football as he thinks he is, he would play for England.'

3

Blackpool
Bound

IMAGINE MY FRUSTRATION GOING OFF TO THE garage every morning. I wanted to be a footballer. Nothing else interested me. The only outlet, just a tiny chance on the horizon, lay in the hands of another Barrovian, Ron Suart, the manager of Blackpool. My father had known him since his youth. I pleaded with Dad to get in touch with him just so that I could have a trial. Deep down I knew that I could make it. My dad was working in Blackpool on and off and one day he went along to Bloomfield Road. Suart told him to take me there. I played a couple of trial matches, watched by the assistant manager, Eric Hayward, and Bobby Finnan who looked after the youth teams. Their verdict was unanimous: 'He's too small. Put

him on steaks and feed him up and bring him back in six
months.'

My parents shovelled the food into me, not that I needed
much encouragement, and every two months or so I would
receive a postcard asking me to play in the B team, usually
with ten other hopefuls. I rarely saw Suart but Hayward,
a big and powerful man, was always around. He had been
centre-half in some of the great Blackpool teams when
Stanley Matthews, Stan Mortensen and Ernie Taylor and
company were around. He was a formidable figure and I
always felt as though I wanted to cower in his presence.
He was always pulling me to one side, often twice in a
session, and he would almost snarl at me, saying, 'You want
to pull your finger out and start playing, because you can
really do it if you want to.'

I couldn't understand why he was always picking on me.
I wondered if he did it with others. Then I convinced myself
that if he was prepared to go out of his way to talk to me
in such a manner then he must have felt I really did have
a chance of succeeding. And I began to try that little bit
harder.

Eventually I moved into digs in Blackpool and worked
at Imperial Garages. My father was convinced that I should
have a trade, although being in Blackpool enabled me to
train in the evenings and so become a part of the junior
teams set-up. It was a vastly different world. At Barrow I
had trained in old and dirty gear. Now I was in a big dressing-room with all the gear neatly laid out and the famous
tangerine shirts and stockings and white shorts for matches.
I did not get to meet the big Blackpool stars – Tony Waiters,
Jimmy Armfield, Alan Ball and so on – because I was working at the garage during the day.

Our training sessions were held at Squires Gate, where
the wind came howling in off the Irish Sea, and if the ball

went out of play it tended to run away for ever or until someone caught up with it.

I was in lodgings with a lovely old lady, Mrs Mawson,
and some other young players, but they seemed to have a
better deal than me. They were full-time apprentices. They
were still in bed when I got up at 7 am to do a full
day's work at the garage. I used to have my sandwiches
at lunch-time, finish work at five o'clock and go straight
to training. Often I would arrive back at nine at night to
eat a warmed-up dinner. I was frequently very tired, but
nothing was too much trouble because I felt I was part of
a professional club.

I was a bit envious of the other lads. I worried desperately
if I would ever be taken on as a professional. The thought
was in my head every single minute of the day. I knew deep
down that I was no boy wonder, and as I approached my
seventeenth birthday there was no comfort in the fact
that very soon they would decide whether or not to make
me a full-time 'pro'. I could not see them keeping me. I
felt that I had not done enough. I was desperate to impress.

Whenever Ron Suart or Eric Hayward were around in
training or in practice matches I used to hope that I could
do something good in front of them. I often look at young
apprentices these days, especially run-of-the-mill lads, and
I know exactly what is going on in their minds. It's an appalling time.

I managed to get into the Blackpool youth side and scored
a couple of goals, then found myself chosen for the eve-
of-the-season public trial match, Tangerines v. Whites.

It was one of those games where everyone has a run out.
I was on the field for the first half and scored a goal against
Waiters. The score is incidental to these matches. They are
staged partly for the benefit of the coaches, but mainly to
let the fans see any new signings and so on. Such public

practice matches have been discontinued by most clubs these days. The big kick for me came the following day when I picked up the *Evening Gazette* and read the four magic words in the middle of the report: 'Hughes made his mark ...' It gave me a fabulous feeling. I was in there. I had actually done something on a football field that had made someone take a note of it. Even to see my name on a printed team-sheet was exciting in those days.

Then judgement day arrived. My father, who had been in Blackpool, told me that Suart would be taking me on as a full-time professional. I wanted to believe him, but I could not wholly accept what he was telling me. I waited for the summons to the manager's office with great foreboding. The walk from the dressing-room to the Presence was about a hundred yards. The manager had said he wanted to see one or two of us, but weren't sure what he had in mind. We were sitting in the dressing-room when off went one of the other young players. The walk takes you along the corridor, past the guest-rooms, along the pitch, through the paddock and into the office. A lot of thoughts pass through a youngster's mind when he's on that route.

This particular day I could hear the lad walking back along the corridor. I wondered how he was feeling. Had he heard good news or bad about himself?

Eventually I made the long trek to the manager's office myself. Suart sat behind his desk. He is a kindly man at most times. He had played for Blackpool and Blackburn Rovers as a full-back. He looked at me and said, 'Well, son, you have been here eighteen months now. We've had a good look at you in the A and B teams and I think we should offer you full-time terms.' He said I would be paid £8 a week.

I hardly heard the figure. Money was of no interest to

me at that stage. I just wanted to be a footballer and he was bringing my dreams to life. I couldn't sign the form quickly enough. I knew that I had two years of proper training ahead of me. If I couldn't make the grade now then I never would.

I was a midfield player and struggled for the first year. I played in the A and B teams and never remotely looked like getting into the Central League side. Often I was twelfth man. One day the left-back in the A team failed to turn up and they stuck me in; a no-hoper playing out of position. I enjoyed the match. In fact I stayed there for four or five matches and then the reserve team left-back, Johnny Prentis, broke his leg. The club policy at the time was to promote from the same position in the team lower down and I was the third-team left-back. My promotion was rapid and there I was, in the last match of the season at Preston, playing for the reserves and again enjoying it. Finnan and Hayward both said, with a heavy sense of relief I suspect, 'At last I think we've found a position for you.'

I had a full year in the reserves. Finally it seemed that my career had started to go forward – and there was every assistance, both vocal and written, from my father.

He used to write to the local sporting Saturday night paper, signing himself 'Seasider' and saying such things as, 'When is Hughes going to get his first-team chance? What a fine prospect this lad looks!' He had other nom-de-plumes such as 'True Tangerine' and 'Blackpool Forever', so that it seemed the clamour for my inclusion appeared to be coming from all quarters!

Reserve-team matches used to attract around a thousand spectators at Bloomfield Road and my father was always there. Only the main stand and paddock were opened for these Central League matches and usually friends and

relatives of the players were among those in the paddock.
He used to walk up and down in front of the directors'
box shouting, 'Hell's bells, this No. 3 is a bit useful, isn't
he? He gets better every week. He looks handy, and they
tell me Thompson is struggling in the first team.'

Despite his claims I stayed in the reserve side for quite
a while but was finally given my chance in the first team
for the last match of the season.

It was 1966 and Jimmy Armfield and Alan Ball had been
allowed to leave early for the World Cup preparations. We
were due to visit Blackburn Rovers and I was brought in
at left-back with Tommy Thompson moving to right-back.
My father had always stressed that first impressions count
for a lot in any walk of life but even more so in football.
I heeded his words. I had to make my mark, something by
which people would remember me because, after all, I was
a complete unknown. Within five minutes I had twice
kicked the local hero, Bryan Douglas, over the touchline.
I was spoken to by the referee and then became involved
with George Jones who had taken a swing at me. We won
3–1 and the Liverpool manager, Bill Shankly, made a bid
of £25,000 for me after that one hair-raising performance.

I was very keen to establish myself as a First Division
player. I knew that Douglas could easily have made a mug
of me. The atmosphere was unreal. I suppose I was diving
around a bit, lunging into tackles. I just wanted to create
an impression. Next morning's papers revealed me as a
killer, a fireball, a rough-house player. It stuck with me for
ages, though as far as I'm aware I've never deliberately
fouled anyone.

But in that match I wasn't happy with the attitude of
three of their players – Mike Ferguson, George Jones and
Barrie Hole, who was a Welsh international. They were trying to unsettle me. They said such things as, 'Get up you

stupid so-and-so ... What are you playing at? ... Who do
you think you are, just coming into the game like this? ...
You want to calm down before someone does you ...
You'll never make a player.'

Hole and Ferguson were the biggest moaners. I wasn't
too bothered by Jones because I knew he had always been
a hundred per cent grafter, but I think he became upset with
my handling of Douglas. I remember going into a tackle
with George. He went down into the mud. It was an awful
night of torrential rain. He picked himself up and at the
same time scooped up a handful of mud and flung it at
me. I wiped it off my face as he ran past muttering, 'I'll kick
you next time.' At the next challenge he dragged me round
and I fell to the turf. The referee ordered him off.

In the eyes of the Ewood Park crowd I was the villain.
They were booing and hissing at me. It was my first experience of crowd hostility but it didn't really bother me. We
came in at half-time, leading 2–0, and as I reached for my
cup of tea I was feeling quite pleased with my contribution.
I wasn't sure what Ron Suart was thinking about my performance. He just looked at me and said, 'You certainly
made an impact out there, son.'

The crowd were going barmy, and their players were
after me. But I was only doing what came naturally to me.
I wanted to tackle. I wanted the ball. I was full of enthusiasm. I could have run for hour upon hour. I would have
been playing the same way had it been an A-team game.

My stamina has always been a strength. During summer
holidays in Barrow, when I was uncertain about my
chances, I would spend long sessions running up and down
the sand dunes on Walney Island, trying to strengthen the
muscles in my legs. I remember how, when I went to Mexico
with the England squad in 1970, the team doctor, Neil
Phillips, remarked on the slow heartbeats of myself and

Colin Bell of Manchester City. The doctor told me that my blood was black!

Anyway, after that first match at Blackburn I went home for the summer. England were winning the World Cup and after it Alan Ball went away to Everton. I was substitute for the first league match of the season and Blackpool were losing 3–0 at half-time when I was sent on. We eventually lost 3–2 but I stayed in the side and never played outside the First Division at any time during the rest of my career.

4

Big Ideas

DURING THE SUMMER OF 1966 I CAME TO REGARD myself as a first-teamer. I had that memorable match at Blackburn under my belt. When I had a letter from the club telling me I was being retained for the following season I did some thinking. I was eighteen and £8 a week didn't seem right for a fully-fledged First Division player. I sat down at home in Barrow with my dad and we decided it was time to take a drive to Blackpool to put our ideas to Ron Suart. The time seemed right, we thought, for my wages to be doubled.

It never once occurred to me that such demands, coming from a youngster with one appearance, could be thought of by some people as outrageous. Suart listened to us, smiling occasionally to himself, and finally offered us £12 a week. With appearance money and other bonuses it was possible for my wage packet to reach a dizzy £30 a week. I had a feeling that Ron Suart was always going to give me a decent rise but he seemed to think it would be a good idea if we worked for it.

I walked out of his office feeling that I had arrived. We set off for the drive home, along the old familiar route we used to travel along after reserve matches. We usually stopped at a friendly little transport café near Garstang on the A6 for a plate of egg and chips, but father had other ideas that day. He drove straight past the café and pulled up in the forecourt of a first-class restaurant just along the road. We called for the menus and 'went through the card'. We were in the big-time now.

Some valuable lessons had been learned in those early, formative years as a young Blackpool player. For instance, Eric Hayward pulled me up one day after saying he had seen me walking home from my work at the garage. He said, 'I saw you walking with your head down and your hands in your pockets and you were dragging your feet.'

I complained to him about early rising, hard work, tiredness, missed meals and my hob-nailed boots.

Eric looked at me and said, 'Listen, son, whether you're a part-timer or not you're a Blackpool player and you should be seen to be proud to be so. It doesn't matter at all that you work in a garage. If you make it into the First Division people will remember you and that's why you must always walk with your head held high.'

Perhaps there were reasons for my tiredness. We were in lovely digs with Mrs Mawson but often there were seven or eight of us crammed into a tiny bedroom – apprentices and part-timers all interested in having a laugh at life. I don't know how Mrs Mawson kept up with our appetites.

We were all growing lads. She had to make sure we were all in bed by ten o'clock and she must have toasted whole loaves of bread for our suppers. But that didn't mean we always went to sleep. We used to talk till two or three in the morning. If any of the lads had been out with a girl we had to know all the details. Had they been to the Tower? Had they danced? We were in camp beds, single beds, some lads even had to share a double bed. Sometimes you had to step over beds and bodies to get to your own place. Whoever was first up used to grab the best sweaters and shirts. Last man up used to resemble a tramp. We shared everything, although the early-riser – me when I was working at the garage – had something of an advantage. There were, on the other hand, some objections to my wearing colourful gear under my oily overalls.

Every weekend when I went home my father used to quiz me about what had gone on at the training ground or at the club. I think he was very worried in case I became trapped by the bright lights of Blackpool. He should not have been concerned; my ambition to be a professional was too intense for me to be side-tracked.

He told me, 'Don't go out now. Stay at home. If you feel you must go out with the lads, then drink Coca Cola. If you go to a dance with them, make sure you're in bed at home by 10.30 pm. Don't smoke. This is the time to be making your career. Everything you want will come to you in the end. You will have cars and money and people's respect and they will wait on you hand and foot.'

It was sound advice and something I could never ignore, although the temptations would always be a distant second to my ambitions. In the summer I used to help with the family business long after I had become a regular first-teamer and it gave me an insight about the way other people have to graft for a living.

The inhabitants of Mrs Mawson's digs changed from time to time and at one spell my companions were Hughie Fisher, a tough little Scot who went on to play for Southampton, Alan Ball and Brian Dean, who, like me, was trying to get to the top. Bally was only an occasional visitor, often staying two or three nights a week but, because the family home was in Farnworth, Lancashire, he could get home most of the time.

We all used to look up to Alan. He had a big red Ford Zephyr and would drive us all over the town. He talked football incessantly. He was Blackpool's golden asset and I was just a young reserve and one clash with him on the training ground taught me a lot about attitudes to the game.

I was playing left-back and Bally was the right-winger opposing me in a practice match. He was very good at playing short passes to a colleague and then darting for the return, making the defending player turn awkwardly. He came towards me, played the ball into Les Lea and went to get it back, but I just managed to get a touch and it broke between Alan and myself. We both went for it; there was no pulling out. I got there a split second before him and caught him a powerful clip on the ankle. He went down in agony.

There was pandemonium. The team's star was lying injured and manager Ron Suart and trainer Wilf Dixon were both on the pitch inspecting the damage. Wilf was moaning at me in his high-pitched, whining voice, 'What the hell do you want to do things like that for? You don't do things like that in practice matches, especially to players like him!'

I felt like a criminal. Bally recovered and the game carried on. A few minutes later the ball broke between us again; I was about to dive in when I thought better of it and he latched on to the ball and was away.

At the end of the move he came back up to me looking angry and shouted, 'Don't you ever do that again, whoever you're playing against. You must always go for the ball. If you pull away like that then there's nothing in football for you.'

I was flattered when I met Wilf Dixon at the Professional Footballers' Association dinner in 1979. As I walked through the room I could see that Wilf was sat talking to Steve Burtenshaw. I crept up from behind and put my hands over Wilf's eyes and said, 'Who is it?' Wilf said there was only one person with such a voice. Then he turned to Burtenshaw and said, 'Of all the years I've had in football there are two kids I've felt privileged to work with when they were no more than children – this fellow and Alan Ball.'

Wilf had seen the way we used to work. I would hang on every word Bally said. He was always keen to improve his game and in the afternoons we would be back at Bloomfield Road, heading, turning, sprinting. I would borrow spikes. I was always a yard slower on the turn than Alan but at the end of two years I had cut down that margin. I used to beg Wilf Dixon to come and have a look at me, to see that I was improving every area of my game. I felt I was gaining in strength and confidence and Alan Ball had a lot to do with it. Just as important was the fact that we were always laughing. Everything was done for sheer enjoyment and that has remained my attitude to the game.

After that Blackburn début, and as I settled into first-team football, there were constant reports linking me with other clubs – especially Liverpool and Bill Shankly. Liverpool were the masters at the time. They had all the great players – Ian St John, Roger Hunt, Ronnie Yeats, Ian Callaghan and so on. They were always contending for trophies; always battling away in Europe; always supplying international players to England and Scotland.

But I was happy at Blackpool. It was the best club in the

world as far as I was concerned. My only interest was in playing football and I would have turned out for nothing if they had asked me. My great loyalty was particularly to Ron Suart. He had my total respect. I knew deep down that I would be eternally thankful for the faith that he, Eric Hayward, Bobby Finnan and Harry Glossop (another youth team helper) had shown, and the knowledge they had imparted.

Suddenly there were rumblings that Suart's position as manager was not so secure. I knew that if he left the club my world would suddenly be empty. Then, and only then, would I allow thoughts of leaving Blackpool to enter my head. I felt that I wouldn't be able to play for Blackpool under any other manager.

And then he was gone. Sacked. The club had been struggling for a while; there had been growing criticism. But his departure knocked a hole in my life. Little did I realize, as I sat in my digs feeling thoroughly depressed, that he still had a big part to play in the rest of my career.

The day after he had been fired I answered the telephone in my digs. It was Ron Suart's voice on the line. He asked me to get up to his house because he wanted to talk to me. I took two buses, changing at Talbot Square, and on the journey my head was full of speculation. Why did he want to see me? Was he joining another club? And, if so, would he be wanting me to go with him?

When I arrived we chatted about the weather and general football topics of the day. He handed me a cup of tea and then began to talk in earnest. I could tell he was building up to something. He told me that I had progressed further than he had ever thought I would. He said he took me on in the first place because he felt he had to give a chance to a boy from Barrow who was the son of a friend. He told me that I had nothing special going for me at the time except a bit of promise. Now, he said, because I had worked hard I was on the brink of a career in which I would be able to make a lot of money.

He is a big, burly honest man and I listened intently. I knew he would never flannel me. I would get the undiluted truth. Slowly he came to the real purpose of my visit.

He said that many clubs had been making inquiries about me. They all wanted to be first to know if ever I should become available for transfer. He said he had thought about the clubs, and my own position, for a long time and had decided that Liverpool would be the best club for me. He told me to be patient, not to say a word to anyone and certainly not to fall out with the new manager, Stan Mortensen. He said he intended to telephone Bill Shankly and that I should rely on him to get things moving. 'Trust me,' said Suart. I would have trusted him with my life.

The longest week of my life passed by, then he telephoned again. He told me to be at his house by eight o'clock in the evening because Bill Shankly wanted to talk to me. I made sure I was there early and Ron and I sat and talked and then the telephone rang. I could hear Ron saying to the caller, 'Yes, Bill, he's here now. Just a minute.'

He beckoned me, and there was that familiar rasping Scottish voice that I was to hear many times over the future seasons. 'Hello, son. How are you?' That question was firm and deliberate. He asked me it about half-a-dozen times and, to be honest, I didn't know how to talk to him. I had heard so much about him that I was frightened of putting my foot in it.

Then he said, 'Don't do a thing. We'll be in for you. It's nice to speak to you. I like the sound of your voice.'

He wound up the conversation with Suart and off I went. I didn't know what to think. The newspapers were full of speculation. I was denying all knowledge of any move. So was Bill Shankly. I was suddenly a part of the cloak-and-dagger business of the transfer market.

But I knew the time had come for me to go. I was not happy at Blackpool. We had played twenty-nine matches that season and had won only one home game. I must be honest and say that I was not fair in my attitude to the new manager. Stan Mortensen was, and is still, one of the most pleasant and affable men anyone could wish to meet, but in my eyes he had taken the job of the man I respected more than any other. I was young and my feelings would have been the same towards anyone who had taken the job.

Fortunately the great transfer soon materialized. Everyone knew I was on my way long before the physical transfer took place. Mrs Mawson was upset because I had become one of her favourite, long-standing lodgers. I was her blue-eyed boy. We were all sat around one afternoon in the digs. It was pouring down outside and Blackpool, on a wet mid-week in winter, is no place to be outdoors. Mrs Mawson came in from answering the telephone and I could tell from the sadness in her face that my departure was imminent.

'It's Mr Mortensen,' she said with a rush of dismay.

Morty was more matter-of-fact when I picked up the telephone. 'Liverpool are here,' he said. 'I would like you to pop round to the ground.'

The next hour or so was pure pantomime. First of all I telephoned my father in Barrow, all of sixty miles away at the end of a wandering, undulating road across the southern end of the Lake District.

He told me to stall things, to do nothing until he arrived. I didn't think I could hold out that long, but I had a good try, and my father must have driven Grand Prix style from home.

I pottered about in the bathroom, having a wash and combing my hair. I hadn't even started shaving at nineteen.

We had a pot of tea and I discussed the implications of the move with Hughie Fisher who said it was a golden opportunity and that I must take it. I put on my Blackpool tie and could not delay my departure for the ground any longer. I did not own a raincoat and as I couldn't get a taxi it looked as though I would present myself before Shanks resembling a drowned rat.

Hughie loaned me his raincoat, which was wonderful of him except that he is four inches shorter than me. It pinched under my arms, I had three inches of wrist shooting out of the cuffs and it was pulled around me tightly as I trudged off to my destiny in the pouring rain.

I turned into the ground and was heading for the dressing-room when I met Shanks standing at the end of the tunnel. He looked at the state of me and said, 'Jesus Christ, I thought you were bigger than that. I thought you were a big boy. I thought you were a six-footer. What am I going to sign?'

It seemed a terrible start, but I peeled off Hughie's coat and he said, 'That's better, you look more like a footballer now.'

We went into a room at the ground and started talking. Stan Mortensen was there and with Shanks was Sid Reakes, a Liverpool director. We talked generally about Blackpool and Liverpool and then Shanks surprised me by asking Reakes to leave the room. He said he wanted to talk to me on my own. I was petrified. I answered him with monosyllabic replies. Then he asked me what terms I would like.

At last I found some inner courage. 'To tell you the truth, Mr Shankly,' I said, 'I delayed coming over to see you as long as I could because I don't want to do anything until my father can get here from Barrow.'

Shanks was impressed. He said, 'Good thinking, son. You get your father here. I like good thinking.'

We waited and eventually dad and my elder brother David, Shanks and myself were together in the room. Once we were all settled and the pleasantries were over Shanks came straight out with it and asked, 'What do you want?'

I said that I honestly had no idea what to ask for. I repeated my Blackpool wages to him in a voice that suggested they were virtually nothing. I said that if we managed to win I could get close to £50.

He looked incredulous and then said, 'How can you pick up £50 when you never win?' I knew I was going to like Bill Shankly.

My father interrupted and said, 'You're signing the lad. We respect you, just say what you want to offer him.'

Shanks didn't mess about. He said, 'I've got international players in my reserve team. I'll put Emlyn on the same money as every member of my first-team squad.'

Before he could come up with figures father said, 'We don't want any more. If that's the truth, and we believe you, that will do for us.'

It amounted to a basic £35 per week, £10 appearance money, £10 win bonus and £2 per thousand people over an attendance of 28,000. At the time Liverpool were pulling in a regular 55,000 and as Shankly said at the time, 'People come from New Zealand to watch Liverpool. And Liverpool never lose.'

It meant that, as a lad of nineteen in 1967, I could be drawing wages of up to £120 per week. It was enough to take my breath away. There was no delay in signing the forms.

I expected I would have two or three days to collect my thoughts and my belongings before joining Liverpool. Not at all. Shanks ordered immediate mobilization. He told me to get off to my digs, pack a case and be ready to travel back to Liverpool with him. 'I want to introduce you to the great Liverpool public,' he growled.

He drove me back to Mrs Mawson's. She had a little cry because I was leaving. Hughie Fisher was delighted to see me making such an exciting move.

The journey to Liverpool turned out to be an unforgettable experience with Shanks at the wheel of his Ford Capri. We seemed to be caught at every set of traffic lights. After the third set Shanks said, 'Aye, so you're joining Liverpool, son.'

'Yes,' I replied, unable to think of anything better.

'Aye, and what colour do Liverpool play in?' he asked.

'Red, Mr Shankly,' I replied, somewhat mystified by his question.

'Aye, you're right, son, and have you noticed that they even make the traffic lights in red?' he said. After a few more sets of lights he was snorting, 'I've had a bellyful of these red lights.'

Now Bill Shankly isn't the greatest driver in the world, and at Anfield they still talk about the day he put his new club car into automatic transmission for the first time and shot straight into the car-park wall.

The drive to Liverpool was not without incident. About two miles out of Blackpool he decided to overtake another car. Then he changed his mind, slammed on his brakes and there was a terrible crunch as the car behind came sailing into us. I felt it was Shanks's fault but he bounced out of the driving seat and was on the attack.

'Where the hell did you come from? What speed were you doing? I'd only just looked in my mirror, the road was clear and then – bang!' he argued.

Looking in his mirror was an irregular pastime for Bill. Anyway he calmed down, they exchanged registration numbers and we set off again with a smashed rear lamp.

It was late afternoon in February and darkness was closing in. We were just driving into Preston when a police motor-cyclist with siren blaring cut in front and waved Bill down.

'Excuse me,' he said to Shanks. 'Do you realize you're travelling without a rear light?'

The reply was fierce: 'You would be travelling with no rear light if some — had just knocked it out! I've just had it damaged two minutes ago. What do you want me to do — not go anywhere?'

The policeman was polite but persistent. 'You're still travelling with no rear light,' he insisted.

At this Shanks erupted: 'You stupid man,' he roared. 'How am I supposed to get home? Do you know who is in this car?'

I thought Shankly was referring to himself and it seemed a rather silly remark. The policeman said guardedly, 'No, I don't know who you are.'

Then Shanks made the stunning observation: 'Not me. There sits the future captain of England.'

I couldn't believe it. I had been a Liverpool player for an hour and we had had one crash, my new manager had been apprehended by the law and he was now talking of me as an England captain. It took some swallowing.

After Shanks had finally dropped me off at the Lord Nelson in Liverpool, a hotel where I stayed for a few days before moving into my digs, I had time to reflect on many happy times at Blackpool. I recalled a televised match against Manchester City which really drew people's attention to my name. I came driving through from full-back on several occasions and sent two shots skimming the bar and had the goalkeeper save a third. Suddenly everyone was talking about the young defender with the scoring flair. I think everyone needs to be noticed if he is going to get on in the game.

There was another incident I could have done without, although I was blameless. We were playing Chelsea in a League Cup-tie at home. Chelsea, managed by Tommy Docherty at the time, were due to become the great team of the late sixties and early seventies. They had a fine collection of young players – John Hollins, Peter Osgood, the Harris brothers, Peter Bonetti, Peter Houseman and company. Peter Osgood was the boy wonder, the star of the show, but it was in this match in a tackle with me that he broke his leg. It was his own fault, though I was considered the culprit and Docherty made an astonishing threat against me.

The incident first, however: there had been a preliminary skirmish when Ossie and myself went for the ball. I tackled him, won possession and he fell into the mud. He rose from the ground looking for trouble. A few minutes later we jumped for the ball in a heading duel and he climbed higher than me. My elbow was in his side and this really had his temper raised.

Then came the explosive moment. I could see him setting himself up to do me as we both went for the ball that was between us but five yards away. I went plunging in because I would not know how to pull out of anything. I went through with the tackle but I could see Ossie drawing back and I thought to myself, 'He's pulling out. He's not going to do me.'

Then I could hear it. I can hear it now. They could hear the sickening snap all round the ground as his leg was broken. Players gathered round. I felt sick because I have never deliberately gone 'over the top' to an opponent in my life.

He was taken off on a stretcher and all our players said that I had done nothing wrong. They confirmed that, in fact, Ossie had been trying to do me but had pulled out

at the last minute. As we left the field at the end one or
two Chelsea players made some caustic comments, but I
met Bill Shankly who had been watching the match from
the stands.

He said, 'Son, you never did a thing. He set himself to
do you and he came off worst for the simple reason that
you're an honest player who went through with your
tackle. You weren't aware of what he was trying to do.'

Truthfully, I wasn't.

We travelled down to stay the weekend in London before
the replay at Stamford Bridge. We won 2–0 at Spurs on the
Saturday (a marvellous result) and were full of confidence
for the replay, two days later.

As soon as we arrived at the Chelsea ground we walked
out to inspect the pitch. The crowd were booing me. They
obviously blamed me for the broken leg their idol had
suffered.

As I was walking off to get changed I saw Tommy
Docherty at the side of the pitch. He said, 'Emlyn, have you
got a second, please?' I thought he was going to tell me
Peter's condition. He looked around as if to make sure no
one was in earshot and then he staggered me by saying, 'I've
told every one of my players that if they get a chance
tonight they're to break your leg.'

I went straight into our dressing-room and told Ron
Suart. He disappeared and came back to say that Docherty
was denying it. We won the match 3–1 and, in fact, none
of their players tried to hurt me. It may have been a crude
attempt by the Doc to put me off my game. In fact it boosted
me. I played well and the result said everything.

Since then I've always got on well with the Doc and with
Peter Osgood; in fact I have 'roomed' with Ossie on many
an England trip.

5

Crazy Horse
Lives

JOINING LIVERPOOL WAS A STRANGE EXPERIENCE.
I knew I was becoming part of an exceptional club. But
how would the other players treat me? Would I be regarded
as something of an outsider? How would I force my way
into such a great team? The side virtually picked itself.

People on Merseyside have had children christened after
the entire Liverpool side: Lawrence, Lawler, Byrne, Milne,
Yeats, Stevenson, Callaghan, Hunt, St John, Smith and
Thompson. In reserve was Geoff Strong, who could fill midfield, attacking and even defensive positions. When I
arrived I was the first signing for several seasons who could
be regarded as a direct threat to the members of that great
side.

I went straight into the team at Willie Stevenson's expense. Willie was a cultured wing-half, master of the long, driven pass. A fluent, attractive player to watch, and taking his place made me realize that I would need to be on top form to justify my selection.

My début was against Stoke City. I went out with Shanks's words ringing in my ears. He said, 'The crowd will hit you with their noise. It will be different from anything you've ever experienced before. I want you to mark George Eastham. Get out there and let him know that you're around.'

Although I had played in midfield as a youngster at Blackpool I had been at left-back in the first team, running up and down the line and never being specifically asked to mark anyone.

Shanks was delighted with my performance. I managed to keep George quiet and we won 2–1. The atmosphere at Anfield that day was incredible. Shankly had been right. It was a brand-new experience to me.

Looking back now I think that Anfield was a noisier, more exciting place than it is today. The crowd has become so used to success that unless Liverpool are really turning it on they tend just to stand and watch. I can remember games around the time I joined Liverpool where we used to pressurize teams, week in week out, so that they were never allowed to get out of their own penalty area. Now, I suppose, there is a tendency to allow teams to play a bit more.

Playing with strangers was not the problem I anticipated. They were all good players and though I struggled to remember names we fitted in pretty well.

Coincidentally, both my father and Bill Shankly gave me the same advice, and it has stood me in good stead. I had been at Liverpool a few days and we were due to play

Newcastle United. Shanks took me to one side and said, 'The crowd are looking for a new name to take to. They need a new hero after the sixties side. They want someone to take over as their own. Go out there and give them something to remember you by. Give them something.'

Before the match I went down to Lime Street station in the centre of Liverpool to pick up my parents. That alone was a new experience. In Blackpool I was able to wander about the station entrance waiting for them without being recognized. Suddenly in Liverpool I was being mobbed. There were hundreds of people in red and white, all wanting to talk to the new signing. When father saw the scrimmage around me he said, 'I thought you were involved in a fight.' As we walked out of the station everyone was chanting my name.

I took my parents to a little café next door to the station, and again I experienced the feeling Liverpudlians have for their footballers. I sat my parents down and walked over to the old lady who was serving, to order poached eggs for myself and a meal for my mother and father.

The old lady was more interested in me than taking the order. She just looked at me and said, 'Ooh, Emlyn, isn't it fantastic, you coming here for your meal!'

As we ate, my father virtually repeated the words Shanks had used. He laid down his knife and fork and said, in a manner that meant I was supposed to sit up and take notice, 'Right, son, you've been here a week. I want you to do something special today. Either belt somebody or make sure that you do something that's out of the ordinary, so that the crowd will know you by it. It's amazing what a crowd can pick up from a player and if they take to you it will stay with you for the rest of your life. No matter what you may do, first impressions are all-important.'

He was drumming the words into my mind and they

stayed with me. I'll never forget that afternoon. As I said, we were playing Newcastle United and they had a forward called Albert Bennett. He was a flying machine, one of those players of whom people used to say 'he's so fast he can catch pigeons'. Maybe, but he wasn't the bravest player in the League by a long way. Half an hour had gone, there was no score and the crowd were getting agitated. As I was playing, the words of Shanks and my father kept invading my thoughts. I knew it was time I did something. My chance came.

The ball was played up to Bennett and I decided to close him down quickly so that he would be unable to get away from me. As I moved in he pushed the ball past me and set off after it when I had anticipated that he would control it. I was done and as he chased after the ball I thought, 'This is my chance.' As he went past I grabbed him by the neck and brought him down to the ground with a rugby-style head-tackle.

It must have looked hilarious. I could hear the crowd laughing because we were close to the touchline. The referee came across and he was laughing as well. He gave Newcastle a free kick and said to me, trying to control his mirth, 'What in heaven's name are you playing at?'

That was the incident that earned me the nickname 'Crazy Horse'. It has stuck ever since. It doesn't sound very flattering, I know, but I have come to like it over the years.

Joining Liverpool with their established players, habits and way of playing wasn't easy at first. I was a bit like an outsider trying to force his way into a private members' club. They were the members of the finest team Liverpool had ever had. The players were not rejecting me; there were no rows, but they had grown up together. They were all close to the thirty mark and I was a lad of nineteen. They were married so I did not get to meet them socially. We seemed to be on different wavelengths at times.

One day Shankly called me into his office. I wondered why. Had I done something wrong? Was I going to be dropped? He sent for two cups of tea; when you went in to see him you had a cup of tea whether you wanted one or not.

'What's the matter with you?' he said.

I was taken aback. I told him nothing was wrong. Everything was fine. I asked him what he was getting at.

He replied, 'You're looking low. Your head is down.'

I insisted that there were no problems, except that I didn't seem to have struck up any real friendships in the team.

That was the clue, the admission he was searching for. He stormed, 'Listen, son, I've seen what's going on. They're not treating you fairly. They don't want to know you. Well, I'll tell you something. If they don't accept you fair and square I'll get rid of the twelve of them. You are the player here now. I'll get rid of the bloody lot.'

I had an awful time settling when I first went to Liverpool. At Blackpool, with Mrs Mawson, I had had a marvellous time. The house was full of young footballers and life was a laugh a minute. When Liverpool put me in the Lord Nelson Hotel, just behind Lime Street, I missed her greatly. I was soon fed-up with living in a hotel room, and after a while I went to Bill Shankly and told him that hotel life was getting me down. My moans registered with him because Shanks always maintained that he hated hotels and because of Liverpool's success he was having to spend a lot of time in them. He understood.

'Don't worry,' he said. 'We'll have you out of there and living with real people.'

He told me he had the ideal person with whom to share digs – the full-back Peter Wall. As it happened Peter was probably the only single lad in the squad who was living away from home. 'The pair of you,' said Shanks with all the promise of a bargain that could not be spurned, 'the pair of you could be Liverpool's next full-backs.'

Alas, it was out of the frying-pan and into the fire. They were awful digs. Tidy enough, but the food was not the solid, reliable fare I had been used to at home and at Mrs Mawson's. Furthermore they had a dog that was rather more than a nuisance.

Peter was not too happy either. We used to call him 'Max' Wall after the comedian, but there was nothing funny in the situation. I became more and more depressed. After four or five weeks I announced, 'Maxie, I've got to get out of here. I can't stand this.'

Often we would spend our evenings at the White City greyhound racing track which was nearby, and there we befriended a young man called Ken Firth. He started to collect us, take us to the meetings and then drop us back home again. One day I told him I had had a bellyful of my lodgings and he surprised me with his response. He said, 'I am only baffled by the fact that you have stayed so long because whenever I have been there I have never felt any warmth in the place.'

I asked him if he knew of any alternatives, any homely people who would take in a footballer. He came up with a cracking solution immediately – his own mother. A quick check with her revealed that there was enough room in the house. I moved in straight away and within a week Peter Wall said he was staggered by the change in me. I was happier, friendlier, brighter. He came and joined us and soon afterwards Alun Evans, signed by Liverpool from Wolves, became the third footballer–lodger under Minnie Firth's caring wing.

It seems unfair to describe the house in Lawrence Road,

Wavertree, as digs. It was more home from home. We were all part of the family. Nobody got preference; not even her son Ken. He took his turn with the rest of us. There was a lovely, warm feeling about the place. We could spread our legs and watch television whenever we wanted.

Peter, Alun and myself shared an upstairs room and, lying there in our beds, we were the best three players in the world. If dreams and hopes won matches and brought fame, then Pele should have given up the game and gone home to Copacabana years ago.

We never went out after nine o'clock on Wednesday, Thursday and Friday and yet Mrs Firth always made sure that we were comfortable. She was a gentle lady, a smashing cook and nothing was too much trouble for her. The only lodger with her now is Steve Ogrizovic, the reserve team goalkeeper who is something of a gentle giant.

There was one incident in training during the pre-season build up. We were playing two-a-side in tight little squares, Roger Hunt and me against Ronnie Yeats and Gerry Byrne. It was mainly a game of keep-ball and scoring goals. Yeats had the ball and I thought it had run out of play. As with all Liverpool training, it was a deadly keen confrontation. I shouted, 'Throw in,' and he answered, 'It wasn't out, man!'

I said, 'Oh, come on, Ronnie, don't be silly – it was out.'

He left the ball, came over to me with fury in his eyes and snarled, 'Don't you ever call me silly again or I'll rip your arm out.'

I remembered the story of how Yeats, while working in the abattoir in his native Aberdeen, was said to have killed a bull with his own hands. I never called him silly again.

Yeats was a giant. The story also goes that when Shanks signed him he invited the press up to Anfield and had them walk around the new signing while Bill talked of him as a Colossus.

My early difficulties were soon resolved when the other players could see, and accepted, that I was a good player. Had I been struggling they might have had reason to grouse, but no one could deny that I was in the team on merit.

Most people realized that sooner or later there would have to be other changes. Alun Evans came into the first-team squad in a £100,000 deal from Wolves and between 1967 and 1970 the game began to witness a remarkable transformation. It was the break-up of a great team, accelerated by defeats in a European competition against the Portuguese team Setubal and an FA Cup-tie against Watford. They were bad results and bad performances for Liverpool.

The Watford match, a quarter-final, was probably the crunch. We were pathetic. We never got started and lost 1–0. I was no better than anyone else. I had been picked for a match against Holland for my first international cap and I remember Shanks saying that my mind must have been on that.

Others lost their places. It was almost the end of the road for Roger Hunt, Ian St John and Ron Yeats. In another FA Cup-tie against Leicester, Roger Hunt reacted in an astonishing manner when he was substituted and, in fact, Liverpool's decision to take him off at Anfield was something that moved me to tears. Suddenly, with the substitute warming up, I saw the trainer signalling to Hunt to leave the field. I couldn't believe it. Roger had always been my hero; a quiet and unassuming man with no temper at all. He had done everything in the world, including a World Cup winners' medal with England in 1966. He was a goal-scorer and a great player. He had done all the things that I wanted to do.

I remember him walking past me as he left the pitch. His face was downcast. He must have been boiling inside because he slowly peeled off his shirt and slung it to the ground in a gesture of disgust. He disappeared quickly afterwards without saying a word. I am sure I was as upset as Roger. As we drove home my father asked me why I was so quiet and saw me wiping my eyes. I told him that I had just seen the end of a legend. And it hurt.

Other players were brought in . . . Larry Lloyd, Alec Lindsay. Ray Clemence and Kevin Keegan were on their way. And although the break-up naturally involved a loss of power within the side it's worth remembering that in the twelve seasons of football when I was a regular first-teamer we were never out of the top five in the First Division.

Bill Shankly had known when he signed me that the team was approaching the top of the hill. They would not be far down the other side when changes would have to be made. However unsavoury that job might have seemed, there could be no time for sentiment.

6

A Lovely Man

BILL SHANKLY IS MY FAVOURITE PERSON. AL-
though he is no longer at Liverpool, and I am playing for
Wolves, I speak to him at least twice a week. He has his
idiosyncrasies, of course. He can be unpredictable in his
attitudes to people, but to those of us who know him he
never changes. He is one of the funniest, serious men I've
ever known. He had a great flair for the language. It was an
economy of words that always took him straight to the
heart of any matter. He was colourful and open and the
epitaph that he has always wanted fits him perfectly: 'He
played the game. He never cheated anybody.' Often he said
things that sounded funny but he was always deadly
serious, until the funny side was pointed out to him later.

My favourite story about Bill tends to confound his belief about non-cheating, but it underlines his immense enthusiasm for football and training.

Shanks was a fitness fanatic. Every day he was at the training ground, moving about, watching everyone individually and collectively. And at the end of the morning we used to split up into two or three five-a-side matches. The most fiercely contested was always the one between the staff – Shanks, Reuben Bennett, Bob Paisley, Joe Fagan and Ronnie Moran – and the apprentices. Once that match had been decided we could all go home.

One day, we had finished but that match was still going on. It got to 12.15, and then 12.45. It was obvious that the boss's team was struggling. We wandered across to watch and stood alongside the pitch when one of the youngsters took the ball round Reuben and knocked it home just inside the post.

I was stood with Chris Lawler, one of the quietest men you could ever wish to meet. Chris was affectionately known as the 'Silent Knight' because he was so quiet. Chris ran after the ball and Shanks was shouting 'No goal! No goal! It was too high!' For these games the posts were two sticks about three feet high and the cross-bar was left to the imagination.

The kids were complaining, claiming that it was a legitimate goal. The argument went on and Shanks decided to call in Chris as an arbiter.

'Here, Chris, you were watching,' he said. 'Was that a goal or wasn't it?'

Chris replied, 'To tell you the truth, boss, I think it just crept in under the bar.'

Shanks exploded. He raged, 'Jesus Christ, son, you've been here twelve years and never said a word. And now, the first time you open your mouth you tell a bloody lie!'

You could usually gauge Bill's mood by the way he walked. Under the old stand at Anfield we were all close together ... dressing-rooms, boss's office, treatment-room and so on. One day as I walked in for training with Ian St John I heard his office door slam and he came walking down the corridor in his side-to-side swagger. I could sense a problem.

'Morning, boys,' he growled. There was something amiss, all right.

'Morning, boss. How are you?' Ian said.

There was no need to prise it out of him. 'Och, I got done with one of those radar traps this morning. And do you know what the crafty beggars did?' he said. 'I was driving down Menlove Avenue and I saw the policeman with the radar so I slowed down. I beat that one and picked up speed again but there was another of the beggars waiting further on and he stopped me.'

He didn't realize that in every trap there was one policeman with the apparatus and another further along to flag you down!

Shanks had remarkable allies in his backroom staff. Reuben Bennett was an amazing man, doing all the hard work and training until he was well into his sixties. Bob Paisley was always around handing out advice and knowledge and often firing some of Shankly's bullets. It was right that Bob should be Shanks's successor as manager.

I remember my first pre-season with Liverpool in 1967. We were playing Cologne in a friendly and Shanks pulled me to one side and said, 'I want you to do a marking job for me today. I want you to sit on Overath.'

Wolfgang Overath was a big world star at the time. He was a midfield creator and had been West Germany's outstanding player in the 1966 World Cup final.

Shanks stressed, 'When he gets the ball I want you to be

breathing down his neck. When he's kicking the ball I want you to be kicking him. In fact I don't want to see him kicking the ball at all.'

I heeded his words and after twenty minutes the ball landed at Overath's feet. I went straight into him. I copped him good and proper and he rolled away over and over again until he stopped as though he were dead. The referee rushed across waving his finger and said to me, 'One more like that and you're off.'

I was a raw youth. I was unaware of the play-acting, the feigning of injury and the gamesmanship that was, and still is, such a part of the game on the Continent. Five minutes later he checked himself into me, fell down and was obviously doing his best to land me in trouble. The referee was waving the yellow card as he came across. His warning was severe and I was aware that any further contact with Overath would mean a sending-off.

Sure enough, as the ball was played up to him again and I moved in, he expertly tripped himself up and went down like a felled tree.

This time I could see the referee fumbling for the red card as he ran towards me. Shanks was on his feet close to the touchline screaming at me, 'Get down!' I fell to the pitch and clutched at a leg that was not hurting.

Paisley was on the pitch to 'treat' and he was saying, 'Are you all right? Don't worry, Overath did you.' Then Bob spotted the red card, put down his sponge and said in a wry, matter-of-fact voice, 'You had better get up, son. You're training in the morning.'

Fortunately, when all the evidence was sifted and the newspaper stories were filed, there was enough support for me to ensure that I did not have to suffer a suspension.

Shanks could be ferocious in his criticism of players, but it was always in private and once he had his say the air was cleared and no grudges were allowed to linger. We have all felt the lashing from his tongue. No adjective or epithet is spared and a player just sits there looking at the floor, unable to lift his eyes to meet Bill's anger.

On one early trip I was having a bad time and Shanks had been moaning to the chairman, Eric Roberts, about my performances. The Press on the trip picked up the theme and although the criticism had been meant for Mr Roberts's ears alone it found its way into the newspapers. It was reported that Shanks had slated me. There was speculation that I might be dropped, or even sold. Wind of it got back to me and I challenged Shanks. His reaction was to call a conference of all the journalists on the trip.

He took me in with him and told them, 'I don't know where you got your stories, and I don't know who has been letting things out of the bag, but you are now looking at the greatest player Liverpool have ever bought.'

I was still only nineteen. It was his way of making up to me. He might well have believed his original criticism. But no Liverpool player could be slated in public without incurring his wrath.

We had some fine encounters with the great West German side Bayern Munich, a team who had several excellent players including Franz Beckenbauer, Gerd Muller and Sepp Maier. We played them two years in succession in European competitions and after going out in the first season on an aggregate of 4–2 we were full of determination the second year.

Beckenbauer had been our destroyer that first year. If you gave him space – and he could usually find his own anyway – he was capable of hammering any team. Although we picked up their forward players Beckenbauer would come through on sixty-yard runs from the back. He had excellent vision and control.

Anyway, the second year we won 3–0 at Anfield and went off to Munich full of confidence. There was just a nagging doubt, though, that Beckenbauer, in front of his own crowd, might just rise to the superhuman heights we all knew he was capable of. Shanks chose Ian Ross, a defender in the centre-forward shirt, and instructed him to keep a hold on Beckenbauer.

He did a magnificent job. Beckenbauer rarely got a kick and Ross even found time to score a goal that put us one up. It looked as though we would become the first foreign side to beat them on their own ground, but close to the end Ray Clemence slipped up and allowed the ball to drop behind him into the net.

We were through, however, and Shanks was raving to everyone about Ross's marking performance on Beckenbauer. 'Ross was magnificent. He could play like that at any level of football in any part of the world.'

He never picked Ian Ross again! That's Shanks.

He revealed to me recently that Don Revie had tried to buy me for Leeds United while he was manager there. The rivalry between Liverpool and Leeds was intense during the sixties and early seventies, although Shanks and Revie often made telephone calls to each other to talk about the game.

Shanks said that Revie had telephoned him at home one day and there was so much small talk in the conversation that he knew there was something else on Revie's mind. Shanks had interrupted the prattle to say, 'Come on, Don, you don't ring me for nothing. What are you after?'

Revie wondered if there were any chance of Shanks taking money or any of the Leeds players in part-exchange for me.

'What did you have in mind?' probed Shanks, who could be a cagey old fox if the need arose.

Revie replied, 'I've got a lad here who's going to be the greatest player Leeds ever had.'

Shanks says he immediately asked Revie why he was wanting to trade him and the Leeds manager replied, 'I think he could do your team a lot of good and I think Hughes could do us a great deal.'

Shanks asked for the player's identity and was told it was Peter Lorimer and that Leeds would be doing a straight swap. When Shanks started to moan, Revie said they might add £50,000 or £60,000 on top.

Shanks ended the conversation by saying, 'If you take Emlyn Hughes I would need Bremner, Giles, Madeley, Lorimer and Hunter – and I would still want cash!'

No manager was more loyal to his players than Bill Shankly. If we were beaten, it was never by a good goal. The other team always won on luck. If somebody took the ball round two defenders and shot into the top corner of our net, that was sheer providence. Nobody could ever play unless he was a Liverpool player. There was one notable exception – Denis Law. Shanks used to drool about him.

He used to say to me, 'I offered £25,000 the first time I saw you play. I eventually got you for £65,000 but if they had asked me for £265,000 I would have paid it. I knew you were mine from the first time I saw you.'

Not all of Bill's moves into the transfer market bore fruit. But he usually had the right response when he failed.

There was the case of Lou Macari. He was a Scottish international with Glasgow Celtic and Shanks was keen to sign him. He came to Liverpool, agreed on the terms, and all that remained was the formality of the signature on the forms. Shanks even brought him into the dressing-room and introduced him to us as a new colleague.

Lou said that, in all fairness, he felt obliged to talk to

Tommy Docherty at Manchester United since they, too, had expressed an interest in him.

When I woke up at home the following day the newspapers revealed that Macari had signed for United. We were in the dressing-room getting ready for the day's training when Shanks came in. We could not resist throwing the papers in front of him with the Macari headlines face up.

Shanks glanced at them and snarled, 'Hell's bells, boys, I only wanted him for our reserve team. He couldnae play anyway.'

Some of the older players used to tell a hilarious story about Liverpool's first-ever European Cup trip to the Icelandic capital of Reykjavik. The party flew to Prestwick in Scotland and, because of fog, were subject to a long delay. To ease the boredom of waiting for the fog to clear and the Iceland flight to take off, it was suggested that the party take a coach for a trip round a whisky distillery. The idea appealed, especially as there was a hint that the odd bottle of Scotch would be handed out. Unfortunately, as the coach meandered among some narrow, fog-bound lanes it became obvious they had taken a wrong turning.

Eventually Shanks, who was sitting near the door, yanked it open and called to a cyclist, 'Excuse me, we are Liverpool and we're on the way to Reykjavik.'

Before he could say any more the cyclist replied, to the amusement of the entire party except Shanks, 'I think you're on the wrong road, pal.'

He hated foreigners. And for all his travel into Europe with Liverpool he never felt at ease. If he stopped someone in the street for directions and they had a foreign accent his first reaction was to ignore them and ask someone else. Nor could he face foreign food.

His hang-ups seemed to stem from the 1965 European Cup semi-final against Internazionale (Milan). Liverpool took a 3–1 lead there and he always maintained they were cheated out of victory in the second leg. Liverpool lost 3–0 and there was some dubious refereeing.

In the build-up to the match there had been a hate campaign directed at Liverpool. The team were met at the Milan airport by demonstrators carrying banners saying 'Liverpool, Savages'.

His general distrust of foreigners showed itself in many ways. During three meetings with the Hungarians of Ferencvaros (six matches in all) he grew to admire their twin strikers Florian Albert and Zoltan Varga. They were a perfect partnership. Albert used to glide with the ball and Varga was the perfect foil. He would take defenders away with him and allow Albert to run at defences. Shanks often used to talk about them, and then one day we were having a pre-match meal in London when one of the lads spotted a paragraph which said that Varga had fled the Iron Curtain. He said, 'Look at this, boss, that Varga has defected to West Germany. He's hopped it from Budapest.'

Shanks took the paper and said with some scorn, 'Jesus Christ, do you mean that he's gone away and left his mate?' He could not imagine them separated.

But there was an acutely serious side to Shanks that showed itself on occasion. He's the sort of person who always writes his own letters to fans and can usually find time for any lame-dog cause. I've seen him moved by sights abroad a couple of times. In Germany we had been driving for hours, through towns and along motorways, and as usual the driver was pointing out the various landmarks along the way. We had to pass close to the site of the infamous Belsen concentration camp. It has been kept as a memorial and inside there are all the macabre sights you might expect. We drove away from the motorway noise and got out of the coach to look at the monument at the gates of the camp. There is now a huge memorial park there.

The atmosphere was uncanny. Although there were trees all around, no birds sang. There was just a deathly silence everywhere. No breeze stirred the foliage. Shanks stood and looked. He never said a word. There was a grave look on his face and I could tell that his mind was troubled.

When we were in Budapest to play one of those matches against Ferencvaros he saw there were bullet-holes in the brickwork alongside a window in a building near our hotel. He asked a guide about them and was told that during the 1965 uprising a pocket of resistance fighters had been holed up there and were prepared to take on the might of the Russians. They had died for the cause. Again Shanks just looked in awe. He was speechless.

With the obvious exception of my father I make Bill Shankly the greatest man who ever lived. He did such marvellous things for Liverpool Football Club and for the people of Merseyside. He built up the club so that they won trophies and with their profits were able to rebuild whole sections of the ground. Everything was geared to winning the European Cup and it was sad that he had already left when we won that trophy two years in succession in 1977 and 1978.

He was proud of Anfield. He loved the Kop. He had a red plaque with the famous Liver Bird and the words 'This is Anfield' written on it erected just over the tunnel where the players run out on to the pitch. It was there when my old friend Malcolm Macdonald came to play against us for Newcastle United. He had not been a Newcastle player long, after being with Fulham and Luton, but he was never short of confidence and came swaggering into the ground with a fancy suit and a flower-power tie hanging loosely from his open-necked shirt. His team-mates were following him and as he spotted the sign he said with some sarcasm, 'Oh, so this is Anfield is it?'

He failed to see Shanks who was walking up the corridor. When Shanks heard Malcolm he boomed, 'You'll soon find out whether this is Anfield or not in another half-hour. You'll be bombarded out there.'

Shanks was never happy with people he thought were clever dicks. For that reason he did not like London or Londoners. He thought that London footballers were softies who spent all their money in nightclubs. I don't think he ever realized that there were nightclubs in Liverpool and that some of his players were their best customers after matches.

We were in London for a match against West Ham a few years ago. The Hammers were having their annual battle against relegation. A journalist came round to the hotel to have dinner and when West Ham cropped up in the conversation the fellow said, 'They are in a bad position. Do you think they'll go down, Bill?'

Shanks responded, 'We might just give them a point tomorrow.'

'How's that?' said the fellow, giving Shanks the chance to make the reply he had so cleverly engineered.

He said, 'If we give them a point tomorrow and they stay up that means we can take four points off them as usual next season.'

Shanks is out of the game now and that, in my mind, is a crime. When I talk to him these days I realize that he is as obsessed with football as ever. I don't know why he retired. I don't think he knows himself. He signed Ray Kennedy from Arsenal one day in the summer of 1974, and the next day he resigned.

His resignation hit me like a shot in the head. I was walking through Liverpool when I saw a newspaper billboard which simply said, 'Shankly resigns'. My immediate re-action was to say to myself, 'Who's Shankly?' I was think-ing of cabinet ministers, heads of government, giants of industry. Honestly, it was several long seconds before it occurred to me that it could be our Shankly. The legend. The team-maker. My mentor. I bought a newspaper and the story sent me cold.

He was the man who had done everything for me. He had taken me from Blackpool and I had gone on to captain my country. Everything I have done is down to Bill Shankly. I made inquiries at Anfield, although it was the close season. It seemed the directors had tried to talk him out of it. John Smith, the chairman, has since said that he walked around for weeks with Bill's letter in his pocket.

The game is missing Shanks. I look around football now and ninety per cent of what I see and hear is unadulterated rubbish. Managers are talking bunk, teams and players are playing rubbish football. And yet Bill Shankly, who has so much to offer in terms of wisdom and experience, has been allowed to drift away. His absence is a crime and everyone in football is guilty for I know that he would like to be back in there in some capacity.

My father made an interesting observation soon after he had met Shanks in those early days when I was being transferred to Liverpool. He quickly sensed Shanks's all-consuming enthusiasm for the game and for players and he told me, 'Don't let Shanks dictate all the time. If you do, he'll crucify you. Argue with him when you know you're right, and back down immediately you sense you are in the wrong. Stand up to him and you'll have a friend for life.'

That is precisely the way I have dealt with Shanks at all times. He is a difficult man to argue with but, after a while, he has always been prepared to see things in a different light.

I'm sure he respects me for standing up to him, though I've had my share of rollockings.

He was always at his best in the dressing-room before a game. There is always tension in the air. It affects players in different ways. Ray Clemence likes to sit in a corner all alone, saying nothing but just staring at the floor. I am a compulsive talker; full of chatter that's really born out of a kind of nervousness which I'm reluctant to acknowledge.

Whatever the state of the players Shanks would walk in and that was a signal for the atmosphere to change. He took the tension out of everyone. He would joke about the opposition, but when we used to run out to face the crowd you could be sure he had started the adrenalin flowing.

He was always good news for any player who was playing badly. There would never be a rocket at half-time, because there was always another forty-five minutes to go. The strongest line he would take with any player who was having the proverbial stinker would be to slap him on the arm and say, 'Hey, come on, let's get going!'

He always preferred to hand out encouragement rather than give a rocket. He produced footballers as well-finished, finely-honed products. Even today, all over the country, other managers discuss possible signings and ask each other the ultimate question: 'Yes, but is he a Liverpool player?'

The lad in question might be with Luton or Bournemouth or a top First Division side, but does he have the grit, the pride and the honesty of a footballer who has been reared the Anfield way? And when Liverpool buy a player they almost always get their money back. In my case they made a profit of £30,000 after having twelve years' service.

Shanks, and later Bob Paisley and the rest of the back-room staff, always ensured that there were no 'stars' at Liverpool. Kenny Dalglish came down from Scotland with a reputation that was sky-high. He was that country's Player of the Year. He had more than fifty international caps and was known as the scorer of countless brilliant goals. But at Liverpool he was just one of the pack, and glad to be so. When he was awarded the Footballer of the Year Trophy he was collecting the greatest individual honour that was possible, but that award had been won by Liverpool players in three of the previous five seasons – Ian Callaghan (1974), Kevin Keegan (1977) and me (1978).

Those early days under Shanks were marvellous for me. I was one of those youngsters who would run all day. I have played at Spurs on a Saturday afternoon, caught the train to Liverpool and then driven north to Barrow late on Saturday night in order to turn out for a Sunday League team. I did that run when I was a current England international. If the authorities had found out I would have been in terrible trouble, but I had so much extra energy that after those Sunday morning matches I was looking for a game of tennis in the afternoon.

I have always loved training and these days I'm constantly sickened by youngsters of twenty-one or so who find it such hard work to report for training on time. They drag their feet getting out to the training ground and complain all the time about being knackered. I just cannot understand young footballers who say that they do not enjoy what they are doing. They are earning good money, they are respected by the rest of the country. Wherever they go people want to buy them a drink or do them a favour. They can go to pubs and discos and every girl in the place is chasing them. They are invited to open shops for a fee or goods, and still they moan.

Maybe I was lucky to have so much enthusiasm built into me at an early age. In those first years at Liverpool people were forever telling me to calm down. Ian St John used to

get on at me for chasing everything to all four corners of
the pitch, but I felt I could do that and always be back in
position at the right time.

I was always getting into trouble with referees. It was
not for dirty play but almost always for the things I said
to them. I have never kicked anyone deliberately in my life,
but I was a devil for querying decisions. Eventually Shanks
took me to one side and said, 'Emlyn, you have been a professional long enough now to realize where you're going
wrong. You're getting referees after you because you're
always on at them. Don't stop having a go, but do it in
a way that will have them helping you. Don't call them
names. You can ask politely, "Why did you give that, Mr
Smith?" Ask them, get them to explain.'

Again it was invaluable advice. For the past six years I
have learned that if you help referees they will help you.
It's amazing how you can earn a referee's respect. I must
admit that since my change of attitude there have been
occasions when referees have given me a generous benefit
of the doubt in some situations.

When I think of all the advice imparted by Shanks, and
when I recall the good habits that were instilled into every
team, I realize that it was an extremely sound decision by
the directors to appoint Bob Paisley as Shanks's successor.
He had been around Anfield for years. He knew the way
we worked. The directors had noticed Leeds United's errors
in appointing Brian Clough, an outsider, to be their
manager in place of Don Revie. Bob, who had been acting
manager, was soon given the job to the delight and relief
of everyone at Anfield. How could you follow Shanks?
Should a new man change the system? Bob was a part of
that system. He let things carry on and that was his strength.
Liverpool were still marching on towards the game's peaks.

In Bob's first season, 1974–5, there was the inevitable spot of readjustment for all of us. We never won anything, which is unusual for Liverpool, but we were regrouping nicely. Bob knows everything there is to know about the game, and with Joe Fagan, Ronnie Moran, Reuben Bennett, Geoff Twentyman, Tom Saunders and Roy Evans in support he had the same backroom team with him.

Tactics and training ticked over as before. There has long been a myth perpetuated to terrify the opposition. It suggests that we train fiendishly and are super-fit, that our training would crease most footballers. That is just not true. Once the pre-season training is over we just go from match to match. The only message that was repeated over and over again was the one first used by Shanks when, in 1962, he set Liverpool FC off on its present course. Then he said, 'Do the little things correctly and the big things will look after themselves.'

7

All In
The Game

THE UNIQUE ATMOSPHERE OF A CUP FINAL NEVER ceases to excite everyone. From the Junior Schools Cup in Barrow-in-Furness to the European Cup final in Rome, there has always been a tingling in the bones, hope in the heart and shuddering in the pit of the stomach that not even experience can prevent.

All the emotions were there when I reached my first FA Cup final with Liverpool in 1971. I was on top of the world. The previous summer I had been to Mexico with the England squad for the 1970 World Cup. Before that I had been on summer tours with Liverpool and with the England Under-23 side, so there had been three years of constant football.

Although we had reached the final it had not been a good season for me. Like most of those players who had been to Mexico and played at altitude I struggled in the First Division. I felt constantly tired. I was falling asleep in the chair at home, something which is most unusual for me. I feel I played only one decent match all season – the last game in the League at home to Southampton. I scored. It was the last match before the Cup final so I began to feel my troubles were behind me.

Our opponents were Arsenal, who were going for the League and Cup double. We fancied our chances. We had been close before. We knew we were as good as Arsenal and none of us were worried about the tension of the occasion. I know I would always play better in front of two hundred thousand than ten thousand. At Wembley there would be the usual hundred thousand screamers and I would back the Liverpool supporters to outshout any other bunch of fans.

It was a hot day. The sun was beating down. It drained all my energy. For some reason we were wearing heavy, thick, long-sleeved shirts. I may be accused of making excuses for my own bad performance, but I'm convinced that our choice of shirts cost us the trophy – especially as we went into a gruelling extra time.

But for all that I have to admit that Arsenal were the better side. We ended up at 0–0 after the first ninety minutes and not one of us relished the prospect of extra time. Suddenly Steve Heighway was on the ball and taking off on one of his runs. Sometimes they seemed like flights of fancy. He was unpredictable. This time he took on the responsibility for our goal, cutting inside a defender and squeezing a low shot under Bob Wilson's body at the near post. One up – I couldn't believe it.

The feeling didn't last long and Arsenal's equalizer

demonstrated to me just how knackered I had become. It was a scruffy goal; a mix-up of players that ended with Eddie Kelly getting the final touch. I could see the ball bouncing about, but my legs just could not carry me close enough to it. The ball ran across me and I knew I should be able to reach it, but the energy that has always been a vital part of my game simply deserted me. I picked the ball out of the net and felt so drained that I could hardly summon the strength to kick it back to the middle.

Not long after, Charlie George collected the ball, jinked inside us and cracked in a shot that was deflected past Ray Clemence. The 1971 final goes down in history as Arsenal's victory. All I wanted to do was get off the pitch. The whistle was sweet relief. I could not wait to get back to the hotel to hide and rest.

The dressing-room was silent. Frank McLintock, the Arsenal skipper, came in with the FA Cup brimming with champagne and invited us all to have a drink. It was a nice gesture but, honestly, one that I didn't appreciate. It only added to the general suffering. We had a swig and thanked him, but the last thing we wanted was to see the Cup being flaunted in front of us. We had some more champagne, and then drank more on the bus returning us to the hotel for the official banquet. When I got to my room I just collapsed on the bed and slept like a child for an hour and a half.

When it was time to go downstairs for the reception for the banquet I was quite light-headed. The champagne had gone straight to my brain and now there was more to drink. I had eaten only one piece of toast all day.

We sat round the table at the banquet waiting for the speeches. There was Tommy Smith and his wife, John Toshack and his wife, Chris Lawler and his wife, and Barbara, my fiancée at the time and now my wife, and myself.

The effect of the drinks showed itself with my impromptu

response to the guest speaker. He stood up and said, 'Ladies and gentlemen, I must say that on these occasions I'm usually invited to the winners' banquet.'

It was more than I could stand. I turned towards him, and in a voice that was something more than a stage whisper, I said, 'Well, why don't you piss off to the winners' enclosure then?'

Everyone heard. The wives were upset. But I couldn't help my reaction. It seemed such a stupid thing to say to so many disappointed losers. I cannot say that I regret my remarks.

At times like that you never think about getting to Wembley again and being winners. But we made it in 1974, taking on Newcastle United.

In the matches running up to the final, two outstanding moments have stayed with me. The first concerned the finest free kick I have ever seen. Newcastle, the eventual finalists, and Forest had to play a quarter-final replay at Goodison Park, Liverpool, because there had been crowd trouble on Newcastle's ground. Forest were awarded a free kick on the edge of the penalty area. Two players ran at the ball as if they were going to play it, but continued running and started a mock argument between themselves away from the ball. With everyone watching their squabble, convinced it was real, Sammy Chapman strolled up and hit the ball into the net. The referee disallowed it on the grounds of ungentlemanly conduct.

Then there was our semi-final against Leicester, a team with whom Liverpool had a history of tense Cup battles. They had a little Irish player called Joe Waters who had been a star in earlier matches. As I watched him struggle I knew that he had been affected in exactly the same way as I had in that final against Arsenal. It is a feeling I wouldn't wish on anyone.

We drew o–o at Old Trafford with Peter Shilton playing magnificently, but there was only one team in it at Villa Park in the replay. Liverpool, with goals from Kevin Keegan, John Toshack and Peter Cormack, won 3–1.

We were off to Wembley, and this time there would be no mistake. The final build-up was different. We had been there before. We knew what Cup finals were all about. We were relaxed. On the morning of the game the TV cameras moved into our hotels. The players gathered round and answered questions about the final through their skippers. I was leading Liverpool by the time and Newcastle's captain was Bobby Moncur. We could all sense that the Newcastle players were edgy. Their nerve-ends were showing. As the interview drew to a close and we were being faded out Shanks chipped in quickly with a remark he hoped the Newcastle players would hear.

'Did you hear that, boys,' he said. 'They looked frightened to death.'

It was a killing, psychological blow. The Newcastle players heard it all right and they played as though they were terrified. Malcolm Macdonald, who had promised all sorts of goal-scoring deeds, hardly had a kick and we won 3–0. We were in fine form and the third goal from Kevin Keegan said everything about our confidence and style. When he put the ball into the net it was the thirteenth touch of a sweeping move.

Princess Anne handed me the Cup. I can tell you now there is no other feeling quite like it. Walking up the steps, raising the Cup high and then being taken round the pitch on a wave of happiness. You just don't want to go in out of the carnival.

We had learned another lesson, too. There were no high-blown speakers at the banquet this time. I had to say a few words myself and while I can't remember many of them I gently castigated the powers that be for not having the trophy inscribed with our name beforehand. They should have known, I said, that after 1971 there was no way we could lose it in 1974.

It was lovely meeting Princess Anne, if only very fleetingly when introducing the players and later collecting the Cup. But I was to meet her again in unusual circumstances.

It was at the first day of the Grand National meeting at Aintree. Princess Anne was there in an unofficial capacity because her husband, Captain Mark Phillips, and Lord Oaksey were to ride the National course after racing, for a BBC film.

I had had a good day watching the racing and was walking back towards my car when I saw Princess Anne and Captain Phillips climbing the gantry up to the BBC TV control tower and interview room.

I said to my wife, Barbara, 'I'm going up there to see what's going on.'

Honestly, I love the Royal Family. I'm a royalist and monarchist through and through. I believe they do more for the morale of our country than all the politicians put together. Every time the National Anthem is played before matches I sing out every word because I believe in it.

When I entered the control tower David Coleman was interviewing Captain Phillips. I nodded across to David, suggesting that he might introduce me.

After the interview David said, 'Emlyn, come over here and meet Mark.'' We shook hands and then Mark introduced me to Princess Anne.

I said, 'It's a great honour to meet you. Actually, we met once before at the 1974 FA Cup final, but I don't suppose you remember me.'

She smiled and said, 'That's funny, because I was thinking that you wouldn't remember me.'

It was a fabulous remark and only added to my view that Princess Anne is a tremendous person.

8

Rain
Saves Us

RAIN, GREAT POURING CLOUDBURSTS OF THE STUFF,
has robbed many a cricketer of his hour of glory. It came
to Liverpool's aid in the final of the UEFA Cup in 1973. The
first leg was to be played at Anfield. Our opponents were
Borussia Moenchengladbach. We had been playing twenty
minutes and the rain was lashing down. It seemed to be
flooding parts of the pitch, but already we had received
other severe warnings from the West Germans themselves.
They were playing well but had one weakness that we
needed to expose. They were employing the great Gunther
Netzer at the back. Brilliant though he was with his feet,
he was not so clever in the air. Unfortunately we had left
out John Toshack in favour of little Brian Hall and had

no one capable of capitalizing on this weakness. I could tell from the start that we would get no joy from Borussia that night.

The rain continued to lash down. Puddles were forming and I was screaming at the referee to get the match put off. He kept saying, 'Give it two minutes,' but eventually he signalled the end and the match went on twenty-four hours later.

By this time everyone had read the script, especially Bill Shankly, and John Toshack was restored to the team. He destroyed them, we won 3–0 and went off to the second leg in Moenchengladbach confident of our success.

For an hour in that return match the Liverpool team took the kind of battering none of us had ever experienced before. They were pulverizing us and Heynckes scored a goal, the like of which I had never seen before. With sheer speed he took the ball down the left wing, cut inside and, as Ray Clemence came to cover the near post, deliberately curled the ball round and away from him and into the top corner. It was a fabulous goal. They scored another to make it 2–0. We were still leading 3–2 on aggregate, which was too close for comfort. But with twenty minutes to go in more pouring rain all their energy seemed to expire. They were gone.

Shanks was wandering up and down the touchline. He was waving his arms. Blowing imaginary whistles and exchanging insults with the German fans who were howling for him to sit down. I thought he was trying to tell us that time was up, but he was letting us know that Borussia were shattered. We did not need telling. We could see it in their faces. We had won the UEFA Cup. There were many more honours to come ... League Championships, FA Cup, UEFA Cup again, and in 1977 and 1978 the European Cup.

I regard the League Championship, which Liverpool

have won five times since the war and a record eleven times in all, as of greater importance than the European Cup. Some pretty ordinary sides have crept through to the final of the European competition. The Benfica side that played against Manchester United in 1968 were a disgrace, yet had it not been for a great save by Alex Stepney moments before the game went into extra time they could have won. Look at the Swedes of Malmo in 1979. They were not even a Third Division side, but if their forwards had been anything at all they would have cashed in on a terrible mistake by Kenny Burns and the outcome may have been something different from Nottingham Forest's dreary 1–0 win.

One of the finest European ties I have ever played in was a quarter-final match in the Champions Cup against the French side St Etienne. It was in the 1977 tournament, the year we beat our old rivals Borussia Moenchengladbach in the final in Rome.

St Etienne had a reputation for fast, open, attacking play. We had the European Cup on our minds now. It had become an obsession in some quarters. But we knew it would be difficult because the French had some good players and had been unlucky to lose the previous year's final to Bayern Munich at Hampden Park.

The match involved a couple of extremely funny scenes. We had heard of their Argentine defender, Piazza, a huge and powerful man who used his size to good effect. None of us had ever seen him play.

We lined up with St Etienne before the walk on to the pitch. I was at the head of the column, Ray Clemence was behind me and Toshack was third in the line. Suddenly I could hear Toshack's Welsh voice above the noise of the crowd, 'Hell's bells. Have you seen him?'

We all turned round and there stood Piazza. Enormous thighs, waist tapered like a ballet dancer's and massive shoulders. He looked like Desperate Dan. He was a giant compared to everyone else.

As we lined up for the kick-off and Piazza dropped back to his position in central defence, Toshack, a big, dry man with a rare humour, strolled up to me and repeated, 'Have you seen him? I'm not going down that middle tonight.'

Sure enough, in almost the first minute the ball goes bouncing between them. Piazza ducks to head it, Toshack lifts his boot to knock it on, but only succeeds in clipping Piazza on the head.

He goes down, his head is cut and Tosh cannot get out his apologies quickly enough. 'Are you all right, pal?' he asks. He is desperately hoping the big man sees it as a genuine accident.

Piazza gets to his feet slowly. He puts his hand to his head and feels the warm blood trickling down. He glowers at Tosh and says murderously, 'Me no okay.'

Toshack comes scampering back at me looking worried. 'He's not okay, Em.'

'Stay out of the middle, Tosh,' I said. 'Right,' he replied. 'I'm going on the wing, Em.'

Imagine all that taking place in the heat of the European Cup quarter-final. But it happened. In fact we should have won that leg. Steve Heighway saw enough of the ball to have won the match himself, but we went down to a last-minute goal from their international forward Bathenay.

We fancied ourselves for the return leg at Anfield, but deep down we knew they were the sort of team to whom nobody could give a goal start.

They came with the right attitude and played some lovely football. But we got a dream start with a goal from Kevin Keegan in the first minute. He broke down the line and his centre from the wing swirled on the wind and over the goalkeeper into the net. A fluke?

Kevin ran back saying, 'I tried it. I tried it!'

I said, 'Aye, I know you did.'

We were now back in the game, although there was still the danger that a goal from them would make it doubly difficult – in the event of a draw the away goal would count double. Bathenay did just that, which meant we had to win the game 3–1 with twenty minutes to go. We brought on young David Fairclough, who was in the process of becoming known as Liverpool's super-sub. Straight away Ray Kennedy scored and we needed one goal to go through to the semi-finals.

Fairclough did the trick with a fabulous goal. He collected the ball in his own half and set off on a run that took him past several opponents. Colleagues were screaming for a pass but he kept going until confronted by the French goalkeeper and then he slid the ball home. We were there!

But, as I was saying, some bad sides do well in the European Cup and the semi-final was a total anti-climax because our opponents, Zurich, were an awful team. They were a goal up early on when Tommy Smith gave away a penalty. Normally, when a foreign team takes a lead like that you don't see the ball for the rest of the game. But they just sat back. After five minutes I shouted to Kevin Keegan, 'Hey, this lot can't play.' He said, 'I know. You're right.' We beat them 3–1. They were scared of us and the 3–0 return victory at Anfield was a dull formality.

9

England In Their Hands

DURING MY CAREER I PLAYED UNDER FOUR different England managers – Sir Alf Ramsey, Joe Mercer, Don Revie and Ron Greenwood. They were all different. They all cared passionately. And I had my moments with all of them.

Sir Alf was in charge when I made my début in Holland. I was left-back and wearing No. 3. On the Dutch side wearing No. 7, the traditional right-winger's number, was Johan Cruyff. Fortunately he operated on the left and did not cause me too many personal problems. An international début is always an ordeal. Although I'd played several matches for the Under-23 side and had been in Sir Alf's

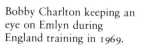

The young Emlyn with his parents and brother David (*left*).

Bobby Charlton keeping an eye on Emlyn during England training in 1969.

And they called him 'Crazy Horse'.

Rivals then, Ken Hibbitt is now with Emlyn at Wolves.

A Goodison goal-post comes off worst as Emlyn scores a goal for Liverpool against Everton in 1969.

Emlyn in action against Wales in April 1970.

Nothing wrong with the left peg.

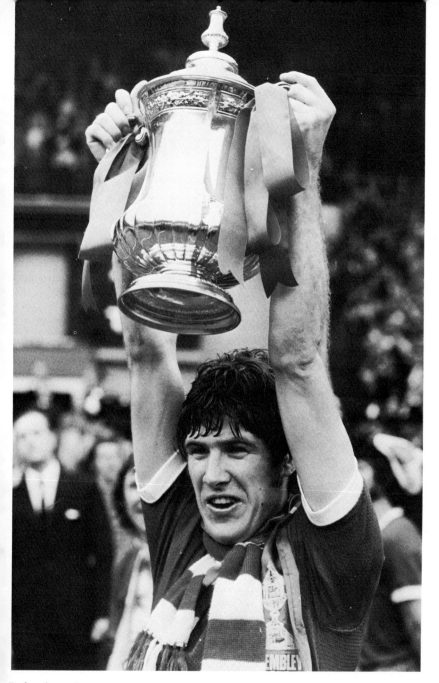
Emlyn shows the FA Cup to the Wembley crowd after Liverpool's 3–0 win over Newcastle.

An extra-time message
from Bill Shankly in
the Liverpool *v*. Arsenal
Cup final.

Warming up before a World Cup qualifying match, Emlyn plays table tennis
with Phil Thompson (*left*) and Mike Channon of Southampton (*right*).

The 1976–7 Liverpool team with trophies.

Emlyn and Barbara Hughes
on their wedding day, 1 July
1972.

Pedal power with Emma.

One of the frequent cele-
brations in the Liverpool
dressing-room.

Emlyn and a great friend,
John Toshack, after the
great win in Barcelona.

The Liverpool captain chats with Princess Anne ...

... and to the Prince of Wales, with Bob Paisley looking on.

For the second successive season, European champions at Wembley after beating Belgium 1–0.

Five of the Merseysiders in the England squad for the 1978 European Championship game with Denmark: (*from left to right*) Ray Kennedy, Terry McDermott, Emlyn Hughes, Phil Neal and Ray Clemence.

Emlyn goes for a run with Red Rum.

The Hughes family today.

squads before, I knew I had to do well. It was the old 'first impressions' routine again.

I came through all right. Nothing spectacular. No rave notices, but a satisfactory début and we won 1–0 with a goal from Colin Bell. As I was walking from the pitch the two West Ham players, and World Cup stars, Bobby Moore and Martin Peters, both came up to me, put their arms around me and said, 'If you keep playing like that you'll be an England regular before long.' It was a magnificent gesture from two seasoned professionals. During the match I had received lots of help from Moore. I was playing alongside him and although he was not the noisiest of people he always had the right word of encouragement for me. If I found myself in a tight corner there was always a word, and he was always waiting to receive the ball to help me out of my fix.

One of my earliest meetings with Sir Alf had been in an Under-23 gathering in Swansea. We were due to meet the Welsh and Ray Clemence, who had not established himself as a Liverpool regular, was to be a goalkeeper. On the day before the international we played a private practice match against Swansea. Ray had an awful time and as we were walking off the pitch Sir Alf came up to me and said, 'Are you sure about this Clemence?'

I told him I was sure of him. He was a good goalkeeper and everyone at Liverpool felt that eventually he would become a regular in the full England side. Ray did not let me down. On that night in Swansea he was magnificent and everyone knows that he went on to become a great international player.

I liked Sir Alf as a manager. He was so loyal to his players that in the end it may have been his downfall. He protected them from every outside influence. And, of course, when the team was doing well no one could get at him. He won

the World Cup in 1966 and could have won it in Mexico
in 1970. He picked me and stood by me when people were
saying that I was too one-footed to be a player at the highest
international level.

Believe me, there are not ten better two-footed players
in the country. I have a great left peg and would use it at
any time. If anything it's stronger than my right, but not
quite as accurate. The criticism probably stemmed from the
fact that when I went off on the overlap down the left flank
I often pulled the ball back so that I could cross it with my
right foot. If this was a failing, so be it, but I was far more
confident of picking someone out with my right. Sir Alf
always said, 'No matter what they say, you'll do for me
at left-back.'

He gave the impression of being aloof and difficult to
many people, but to his players he was magnificent. He was
a friend. We never called him 'boss' or 'sir'. To us he was
always Alf.

Not that anyone ever took any liberties. He could be a
master of the put-down if he thought someone warranted
the treatment. I remember his attitude towards me after one
of the group matches in the Mexico World Cup. England
had beaten Czechoslovakia and although I had not played
we were all told that we could go out but must be back
in our rooms by half-past midnight. A Polynesian-style bar
down the road seemed to be the ideal place for a few of
us.

I telephoned my mother and father who were in Mexico
for the tournament. My old Liverpool pal Roger Hunt,
who was over as a travel-firm courier, used to joke that my
father had come to watch me sit on the bench. He wasn't
interested in the play!

My father came and joined us and, of course, by 10.30
pm he was putting the team to rights – I was the first name

he pencilled in – and when he left at 12.30 I was beginning to feel sorry for myself. By this time other players were drifting in and we had a couple of drinks before going to bed at about 1.30 am. Nothing was said at breakfast, but then Harold Shepherdson, the trainer, said he had heard that Sir Alf was not too happy with one or two of us. I guessed the worst.

As training started, Sir Alf just said simply, 'Emlyn, I would like a word with you when we've finished.' I was petrified. All of a sudden I could see myself being sent off to England on the next plane home. I could imagine the fuss. Reporters would be waiting. I would be known throughout the game as a bad lad. I felt like a criminal and he was letting me stew through a full morning's training before handing out the punishment.

A couple of other lads who had been in the bar were getting the same treatment. I had seen Sir Alf pull them to one side. Their heads dropped; the enthusiasm disappeared from their training.

Eventually, as we left the field, he came alongside me and said, 'What were my instructions last night, young man?'

I said, 'You're right, Alf. I was out of order. But surely you must understand how I feel. I'm here, and you know how much I love the game and how keen I am, how much I want to play.'

He looked at me coldly and replied, 'I understand your feelings perfectly, young man. I pick the team. I pick the subs. I'm the boss of this outfit. You'll do as I say or, believe me, you'll be on the next plane home. Now piss off.'

I said, 'Look, Alf, I have let you down. I really am sorry. It won't happen again.'

He said, 'Son, you haven't let me down. But if any of the journalists had been just a little bit naughty they could have written a hell of a story about England players drinking after a curfew. You would only have let yourself down.'

He was right ... a lad of twenty-two on his first major international trip abroad breaking a curfew.... The thought of the headlines that might have been still makes me shudder. I was relieved just to get away with a rollocking.

Mexico was a fabulous experience, but not without its anxieties. At first Sir Alf named a squad of forty. Then it was whittled down to twenty-eight for a pre-World Cup tour of Colombia and Ecuador. Then he had to name his final twenty-two. Every time he came to a decision I felt sure I was going to get the chop. I felt desperately sorry for those who did not make it. My old friend and rival from Everton, Colin Harvey, was one of those who did not make the touring squad. Then my clubmate, Peter Thompson, missed the final twenty-two. He stayed on with David Sadler as a non-playing member of the squad while the four other disappointed men – Brian Kidd, Peter Shilton, Ralph Coates and Bob McNab – chose to go home.

I would have stayed on. The experience of seeing so many fine teams and players seemed to me to be too good to miss. Although I did not play I enjoyed the whole trip. You learn so much about football and even Sir Alf's lecture did me a power of good.

Of course the trip started off with that celebrated, but concocted, charge against skipper Bobby Moore that he had stolen some jewellery from the hotel shop in Bogotá. In the shop all kinds of trinkets, rings and bracelets were laid out and we were encouraged to browse because we were told that the gold was very good value. In fact, I bought Barbara's engagement ring there.

In the shop everyone wanted to talk to, and touch, the great stars such as Bobby Charlton, Bobby Moore and Alan

Ball. People were taking pictures of them but soon we had either bought all we wanted or had finished looking. We were walking out when suddenly a man came rushing out shouting, 'Police! Police!' Next thing we knew Bobby was going off for questioning although everyone in the party knew that to have stolen anything would have been impossible. Sir Alf kept cool and we left for the Mexican tournament without Bobby. Fortunately we were all readily aware that he was a strong, cool customer who would not crack under pressure.

Before then we had never played at altitude; it was our first experience of the difficulties such conditions presented. If anything it should have been easier for Colin Bell and myself. We had shown, through heart-beat and pulse-checks, that we had an advantage. I had never been fitter in my life. I carried not one ounce of spare flesh. I found that in Colombia and Ecuador I could run faster than ever. That wasn't the problem – the business of recovering was the crippler. I would go off on a run down the field and only begin to feel the pain when it was time to get back to my position. The oxygen had gone from my body. I was gasping for breath. My ribs were heaving in my sides like a greyhound at the end of a half-mile sprint. I could not speak to any of my team-mates, and I knew they were all feeling the same. In one match I lost half a stone and when you remember that I was carrying no extra weight that was an amazing amount to lose.

That part of the trip was another brief encounter with the histrionics of the Latin American footballer. When he is injured he resorts to the uniform Dying Swan act. The agony, the rolling over, the facial contortions ... at times they were exaggerated enough to be comical. Then, of course, the horns and hooters created a fearful din.

England's reception in Mexico was hostile, to say the least. We arrived as world champions, but it seemed that England had few friends in Central America.

I have no intention of criticizing Sir Alf, but he probably underestimated the importance of public relations in such a situation. As far as he was concerned we were there to play in a football tournament, and he was quite right. But the Mexicans were upset because we had taken our own bus and much of our own food. Why not? It was taken as an insult by the locals, but we were only trying to be thorough and to keep our match preparations as normal as possible. Meanwhile other countries, the Italians, the West Germans, the Brazilians and so on, were going out of their way to be seen in the right light. They were pictured holding babies, posing with Miss World and generally being friendly with the natives.

Looking back now I can see the Mexican viewpoint, but I can also see Sir Alf's, and if I had to take a team there myself I know I would do it his way.

The height of Latin American hostility probably occurred on the evening before the vital match with Brazil. The fans – naturally the locals took Brazil's side – began their rumpus outside the Guadalajara Hilton, where we were staying early in the evening. It was obvious there would be trouble. We had been warned. I was sharing a room with Peter Osgood and Peter Thompson. I was the only one directly involved in the following day's match, being one of the substitutes. At some stage during the evening I went to get myself a drink and completely missed the hurried re-arranging of rooms that went on. All the players and substitutes were to be moved to the back of the hotel where it would be quieter. I slept at the front – or tried to sleep.

All night the circus went on. A deafening parade of

whistles, drums and trumpets. It sounded like a thousand West Indian cricket supporters in full cry.

Some of the lads declared war on the rabble below. They emptied a milk machine of its cartons and bombarded the mob. Buckets of water rained down. But it was a steamy hot night and the invaders didn't seem too worried. In the end we could only joke about it.

The incident between Peter Osgood and me a few seasons earlier had been long forgotten. We shared rooms many times on England trips. Ossie was always great company and we never mentioned the day of his broken leg at Blackpool.

The match was something of a crunch. We were the World Cup holders and Brazil, with Pele back to form along with such giants as Gerson and Tostao, were favourites – a position they fully justified with a marvellous win over Italy in the final.

Conditions for the Brazil match were cruel. It was a noon kick-off in order to accommodate world-wide television. The temperature was in the nineties and it was bad enough being a sub, let alone out there playing.

As a left-back I watched from the side, keeping a careful watch on Terry Cooper who was in that position and facing Jairzinho, a fast winger with the stealth of a panther. A couple of times he went round Terry – once to provide the centre from which Gordon Banks made that unforgettable save from Pele – and I found myself telling Terry which way Jairzinho would go. Maybe it's easier from the side, but I couldn't help thinking that had I been out there I would have played him better and he might not have been given all the room that allowed him to cut in for Brazil's winner.

England were unlucky. They matched Brazil in everything. Bobby Moore was majestic.

International players in those days were always on promised 'boot money' from rivalling manufacturers. If you were seen in action wearing a particular boot you collected £100. The subs formed a deal of their own. We paired off so that if your partner got on to the pitch you shared the money. The goalkeeper, in this case Peter Bonetti, was on his own and would be able to keep his full whack.

I thought I would be a bit shrewd and chose Nobby Stiles as my partner. I reckoned if anyone would be sent on it would be Nobby, especially if we needed someone to get out there and make his presence felt in the time-honoured way. The other subs were Jeff Astle and Colin Bell. They went on, collected £100 apiece and left Nobby and me with nothing.

Still, we were through to the quarter-finals and there were many teams now beginning to fear us. The Romanians and Czechoslovakians had been defeated and the match against Brazil had shown that, despite the 1–0 defeat, we were every bit as good as them. We had players they all envied ... Gordon Banks, Bobby Moore, Bobby Charlton, Alan Ball. All men with towering reputations.

The quarter-final was to be played at León, a distant town away over the Sierra. On the way Gordon Banks was pale and ill with a stomach upset. We were not too concerned. The England doctor, Neil Phillips, had taken every precaution and we assumed it was some disconcerting little bug that would pass on in a matter of hours.

Banks was the greatest goalkeeper in the world. He was unlikely to miss a World Cup quarter-final with a stomach upset. There was no concern when he missed light training and when he turned up at the team meeting before the match I guessed everything would be all right. We had a light meal, went to collect our things and on the way to the coach Alan Ball told me that Banks would not be playing and that Peter Bonetti would be in goal. To say it was a blow is the understatement of all time. It seemed that the excitement of getting up to prepare for the match had knocked him out completely.

Maybe Gordon's illness put some extra resolution into the rest of the team. There were no qualms about playing Peter. After all, he was known as 'the Cat' because of his extraordinary fitness and agility.

England played brilliantly in conditions that were no less difficult than in the Brazilian match. Two magnificent goals from Alan Mullery and Martin Peters seemed to have England safely through to the semi-finals.

But no. Beckenbauer scored for West Germany and England took off Bobby Charlton to replace him with Colin Bell. Ten minutes to go and England, still leading 2–1 sent on Norman Hunter in place of Martin Peters. Almost immediately West Germany equalized and in all the agonies of extra time they scored the winner.

Recriminations galore surrounded the England camp. Sir Alf was slated because of his substitutions and Peter Bonetti was faulted for his goalkeeping.

I rise to the defence of both men. Sir Alf did what any other sensible manager would have done when he took off Bobby and Martin. We were 2–0 up with twenty minutes to go. Bobby, who was getting on in football terms, would benefit from the rest as England looked set for a semi-final date. Martin, who had grafted non-stop in the heat, was suddenly looking tired and his replacement, Norman Hunter, would surely strengthen midfield. The team were playing well and there was no reason to believe that everything would suddenly fall apart.

Nor do I blame Peter Bonetti. What happened in front of him? What happened to the back four? Or the people in front of them? Looking back, the match seems to have been recorded as a catalogue of Peter's mistakes, but I believe the people playing in front of him were not entirely blameless over England's exit from the 1970 World Cup.

In the dressing-room the atmosphere was funereal. Everyone was stunned. Players and substitutes and officials just sat around. Alan Ball was crying. Sir Alf moved around trying to pick up people's spirits, thanking them for their efforts and telling them all that they could not possibly have done any more. Peter Bonetti was taking it worse than anyone. I felt very sorry for him.

An even bigger, black cloud of despair was to settle over Gordon Banks as he lay in his darkened room at the hotel. He was watching the match on delayed transmission television. The programme, showing the whole match, started one hour after the official kick-off time.

He was lying there with the set on when Alex Stepney, his room-mate, returned after the match. England were winning 2–0 as Alex walked in and Banksie, cheered by the play, was shouting and feeling much better. Alex broke the news. We had lost 3–2.

Banksie couldn't believe it. He did not want to believe it. He accused Alex of making sick jokes. But by the time the rest of us arrived he could tell by our faces that 3–2 was the awful truth.

We held a wake at the hotel and it went on most of the night. A certain false defiance was in the air. Sir Alf said we could stay and watch the rest of the tournament, but we all decided that it would be better to get home and out of it.

There was still the 1974 World Cup to come. I had not played at all in the 1970 tournament and to play in the greatest international competition of them all was among my ambitions. We were drawn in a qualifying group with Wales and Poland.

The home draw against Wales was a blow early in the qualifying rounds, but defensive mistakes by Bobby Moore and then by the man who replaced him, Norman Hunter, against Poland at Wembley, gave the Poles the goals that carried them through one point ahead of England in the group table.

The Wembley match against Poland was really Sir Alf's do-or-die game. We came agonizingly close to pulling off a victory and no one suffered more than poor Norman Hunter. For years he had been a star of the Leeds United side but had been kept out of the England team by the immaculate form of Bobby Moore. As the ball broke into England's half with the score o–o, Norman reached the ball. Normally he would have slid it out of play. Instead, he tried to put his foot on the ball before playing it gently back. Something went wrong and Lato burst on the ball and was clear before providing Domarski with the goal. We pulled the goal back with a penalty from Allan Clarke, but could do no more.

The Polish goalkeeper, Jan Tomaszewski, had all the luck in the world and I will never know how he kept out a shot from Kevin Keegan right at the end. But, when all the shouting had died and the inquests were over, England were out of the World Cup and the daggers that had been aimed at Sir Alf's back for some time now went straight in.

He left the job and I was among those saddened to see him go. I suppose it was inevitable. Failure to qualify was looked upon as a crime. Although the players had faith in Sir Alf there were obviously many other people in the game, as well as Press and public outside the game, who had lost faith in him. When things are going wrong the spirit in the squad tends to die a little.

It was an inspired choice when the FA announced that Joe Mercer would be caretaker-manager for the 1974 Home

Championships and the East European tour of East Germany, Bulgaria and Yugoslavia. Joe came breezing in and everything was done for a laugh. Whereas Sir Alf had done everything correctly and straight down the line, Joe had little time for formalities. He was just what the team needed at this particular time. I had known Joe for a long time. Some of the lads were not so sure and I wondered how he would make out.

The members of the squad first met Joe on a training pitch in Wales before the international match. He gathered us round him in a group in the middle of the pitch and his opening remark was, 'I didn't want this bloody job in the first place.'

That broke the ice. It was a very important moment and it somehow let the lads see that we would certainly not be dealing with a 'flanneller'. If he had started laying the law down about tactics and discipline he might have lost our support and respect at the outset.

We knew his record, of course. He had been a wonderful wing-half with England, Everton and Arsenal. He had managed Aston Villa and Sheffield United and had been the influential senior partner with Malcolm Allison during some of Manchester City's greatest days. But he was now a Coventry City director and was getting on a bit in years.

His second statement to us that morning in Wales was, 'We're all going to have a laugh and a joke these next couple of weeks.'

Laugh and joke we did. A wonderful, friendly atmosphere prevailed throughout the home internationals and the tour. During training before the Welsh match Joe came up to me and said, 'What do you think of the lads?'

I replied, 'All right, Joe.' I wondered what he was getting at.

Then he said, 'Is there anyone else you think should be in the squad?'

I was puzzled and replied non-committally, 'I don't know, Joe.'

He said, 'If you can think of anybody let me know and we'll get them in. You'll have to become involved in it because you're going to be my skipper.'

It suddenly dawned that I, the great patriot, was to be captain of England. It was another dream come true.

We defeated Wales 2–0 and from then on Joe seemed to consult me about everything. He made me smile one day when he brought up the subject of Micky Pejic, who was playing at left-back.

Joe said, 'What do you think of Pejic?'

I replied, 'He's all right, Joe. He's okay.'

I could see that Joe wasn't really interested in my response this time. He just said, 'No. Definitely not.'

I asked him to explain and he said, 'He doesn't effin' well smile. I'm not having him in my team if he doesn't smile. We'll get Alec Lindsay in.'

He sent to Liverpool for Alec to join the tour party in London before setting off for Leipzig and he went on to play in all three games. I did not altogether enjoy the choice of countries we toured. Most of us hardly saw outside of our hotels, apart from training and playing. Bulgaria was probably the worst. The hotel was poor and the moment anyone stepped out of the front door he was mobbed by people asking for ball-point pens or money.

We were glad to get out of there but only into an international incident at the next stop, Belgrade Airport, Yugoslavia. It was here that the Kevin Keegan fiasco occurred.

Kevin is a great little chap, one of my best friends. I had shared rooms with him and played cards with him. After we had landed, our bags were sent down a chute. Alec Lindsay had put his suit-hanger on top of his case and saw that his coat-hanger had become caught up in the mechanism. It would not dislodge itself and Alec could not move it without being in danger of tumbling into the chute himself. There was only one thing to do. I held one of Alec's legs and Kevin held the other as he reached in. We helped him out and were moving through to the baggage reclaim area when a couple of policemen grabbed hold of Kevin and started to lecture him.

Naturally Kevin tried to shrug out of their grip and asked them, 'What's going on?' It was a thoroughly bizarre scene. He had done nothing wrong. Suddenly two of them got hold of him firmly and rushed him into a room, slamming the door behind them. I dashed off to tell Joe Mercer and by the time the FA officials came through to see what had happened Kevin had been allowed out of the room. He had been beaten up and was very upset. They had made him kneel in front of them while they hit him.

The outcome was that the Yugoslavs tried to smooth things over, saying there had been a misunderstanding. On ensuing tours and England trips, however, the FA insisted that the players dress like a team, even if casually. I think they were right to make this decision because I suppose we were dressed in a collection of tee-shirts and denim trousers. Frank Worthington, his head-band, Harvard University shirt and transistor radio plugged into his ear, hardly looked the international footballer passing through an airport.

It was a very unfortunate incident on what turned out to be an excellent tour. The players had been allowed to play their own way in the matches. Whether things would have remained the same had Joe carried on, no one will ever know. But it's doubtful that England could ever have approached World Cup or European Championship matches with such a cavalier attitude.

I have always admired Joe and my estimation of him went up as a direct result of that tour. He remains one of football's finest elder statesmen.

When Don Revie became the England manager I felt that England had gone for the right man. He had done marvellous things with Leeds and, while they had not always been the First Division's most popular side away from Elland Road, most people recognized that he had done a thoroughly professional and tactical job. I also reckoned that my own international position must be fairly secure because he had once tried to buy me.

His first move was to invite almost a hundred potential England players to a weekend gathering at the Hotel Piccadilly in Manchester. He told me I was to be his captain and everything was looking good.

The relationship started well. And then suddenly, during the 1975 home international championships on the night before the match against Wales, he called me to his room at the England hotel in Cockfosters, London, and said, 'I'm not picking you for tomorrow's game and I will not be needing you in future.'

'Why?' That was all I could think of to say.

He replied, 'I'm thinking of the future and I'm going to build around certain players. You are not one of them.'

I was stunned. I could see it was pointless arguing or even having any further discussion. He had made up his mind. I stood up and said, 'Thank you. Fair enough. I've had a good run.'

But I went back to my room in a state of disbelief. Kevin was there, of course, and I told him what had happened. He took some convincing that the conversation had actually taken place.

Soon afterwards the England doctor, Dr Burrows, came on his round of the rooms offering mild sleeping tablets to anyone who wanted to be sure of a good night's sleep. I usually took one the night before a match.

I said, 'Yes please, Doc – for the last time. I won't be seeing you after this because the manager isn't going to pick me any more.'

He laughed. 'There you go, always trying to be the joker.' He left, obviously not believing a word I had said. Who could blame him? After all, I had been a regular member of the England squad for five years and I was still only twenty-seven. Hardly an age to be tossed on the scrap heap. I went along to watch the game and stayed with the squad until after the Scotland game on the Saturday. It was an awful time for each new day brought the deeper realization that it was all over.

There had been a whisper that Revie suspected I had been something of an accomplice when Kevin Keegan had defected from the England camp before an earlier midweek international. At the time Revie had said he was going to try some different players – he was choosing some no-hopers at one stage – and when Kevin was left out he was hurt. As usual I was sharing a room with him and did my best to get him to see sense and stay.

He came in one night and said, 'That's it. I'm off!'

I said, 'What do you mean? Off?'

He told me he had seen the team. He was not in it and he was going home to Doncaster, his home town.

I tried to reason with him: 'Look, Kevin, he has explained the reasons for his team selection. Sit down, and before you do anything daft just think about your England career. It's only just beginning. You have every chance of being the greatest player England has ever known. Just go and have a chat with him if you feel so bad.'

He was adamant. He said he was not going to stand for it. He just packed his case and left. Short of physically restraining him – and he's as strong as an ox – there was nothing else that I could do.

I went to see Revie and told him exactly what had happened. He told me to say nothing to anyone and that he would break the news later on. It seemed that even then he was trying to think of a cover-up story.

Revie found it difficult to switch from being a club manager to an international manager. He tried to create within the England squad the atmosphere that prevailed at Leeds. That is fine when you are with the same group of players every day, but taking lads from all over the country for brief periods does not always draw the same response.

I was not one for the regular organized evening sessions of bingo, carpet bowls and putting. I think he could sense that some players didn't like being dragooned in this way. I always took part because I felt that, as captain, it was right that I should, but it's possible that my reluctance showed through.

Two years and fifteen international matches later he had to bring me back because he needed my experience in central defence for the World Cup qualifying tie against Italy in Rome. I did not enjoy my exile from the international scene.

I was at home in Formby one Sunday morning when the telephone rang and Liverpool manager Bob Paisley was on the line. I wondered if Bob had a problem he wanted to talk about. Then he told me that Revie had spoken to him a few minutes earlier and that he wanted to call me back into the squad. I laughed and told Bob I did not believe him. Bob knew I had been very hurt about being left out. He told me that Revie would call me at home between five and six o'clock that evening. Then Bob stressed, 'Whatever you do, and whatever you say, don't lose your rag. You're the easiest fellow in the world until you start shouting. So remember, don't lose your temper.'

I promised that I would not. Then I telephoned my mother to tell her the news. The next person I telephoned was my great friend Bob Moss, the man who ran my testimonial at Liverpool, who lives just down the road. He asked me to pop down for a glass of champagne in celebration. It was 10.30 on a Sunday morning. Barbara was with me, and two other friends, and between us all we had thirteen bottles of champagne. By five o'clock I was just ready for him. I was full of bravery after a few glasses.

The telephone rang and the conversation went like this.

'Hello.'

'Emlyn, it's the boss here.'

'Who?'

'The boss ... Don Revie.'

'Oh yes. How are you? The boss, Bob Paisley, rang to say you were going to telephone.'

'I'm ringing to tell you that I'm going to include you in the squad for the Italy match.'

'Don't do yourself any favours, will you? Why are you including me now when you've left me out for fifteen internationals? There's not a better centre-back in the country than me, and hasn't been for some time.'

'I didn't think you would have taken this attitude, son.'

'Attitude? What about your attitude? You've seen me play. I played at Wembley at the start of the season in the Charity Shield and never gave your blue-eyed Southampton boys a kick.'

'I think your attitude might just be a little bit wrong, son.'

'Why do you want to pick me now? You've been playing rubbish in all sorts of positions and but for you leaving me out I would be the fourth most capped player in history.'

The bad feeling was pouring out of me. Barbara took the children upstairs out of the way. Out of the corner of my eye I could see her shaking her head. 'You're going to blow it,' she was telling me.

Revie said, 'I will see you when the squad is announced.' And with that he was gone off the line.

I calmed down a little and suddenly I knew I had to talk to Bill Shankly. And I knew that I had to apologize to Revie. As I wondered what move to make first I remembered something that Shanks had always said when I became het-up about anything. He used to say, 'Emlyn, I can always handle you but I never want to talk to you when you are annoyed. Then it's impossible.'

I telephoned Shanks, told him what had happened and asked him for Revie's home number in Leeds. I was looking up the STD code for Leeds when Revie rang again.

His opening statement was chilling enough to go straight to my heart.

'I have been thinking, son,' he said. 'I'm not going to name you.'

That was a knock-out blow. I almost burbled my response and said, 'To tell you the honest truth I have just put the phone down on Bill Shankly. I asked him for your number so that I could call you to apologize. I got a bit carried away. Give me credit for the way I think. I've been playing the best football of my career over the last two years.'

He was listening. I could sense he was mellowing. I went on: 'I do apologize for the way I carried on, but you must understand the way I felt. When the boss told me you were including me I went and had a couple of glasses of champagne with some friends and I was just a bit excitable.'

He said, 'Let's leave it at that and I will see you when the squad assembles. We can have a chat then.'

I said, 'I won't let you down.' Then I hung up before he could change his mind.

When I met up with the squad in London Revie welcomed me as though I had never been away. But I know that I will never have any real respect for the man again. There was never any explanation about why he had left me out or why, indeed, he had brought me back.

He chopped and changed the side so much that we used to have a standing joke: if you had a bad match you said to the lads, 'See you in the League.' If you did not do well you were left out, whereas Sir Alf Ramsey, and currently Ron Greenwood, believe in persevering with players who may be temporarily out of sorts.

My period of exile coincided with the era of the massive dossier. Fortunately Revie had dispensed with them by the time I returned to the England side.

To be fair to Don Revie I have met him since and he has been marvellous with me. Once I was in Dubai in the United Arab Emirates to play a friendly match with Liverpool and when we arrived at the hotel he came straight to me before the officials. He shook my hand and said, 'You proved me wrong, not once but three times. I'm delighted for you and can only say that I'm sorry for what I did to you.'

The manner in which he left England high and dry was underhand and pathetic. He missed the start of the 1977 South America tour (Brazil, Argentina and Uruguay) because he said he wanted to watch Italy play Finland in a World Cup qualifying match. In fact he stayed behind to negotiate with the Arabs so that when he flew into Buenos Aires to link up with us he knew that he would soon be leaving.

This was his dark secret. We had not missed him in Rio, because the atmosphere had been the most relaxed I had known it under his regime. Les Cocker, his faithful assistant who was to join him in UAR before returning to Doncaster Rovers (where, sadly, he died in 1979) let us do our own thing. We frolicked in the surf. We swam in the pool. I played tennis before breakfast with Gordon Hill and Trevor Francis. There was no bingo and the spirit was good.

By now, of course, the man-on-the-terrace was convinced that Revie's reign was over, even though no one had an inkling of his intentions. When he left I felt he had let down his country. We no longer had a regular England squad – only Ray Clemence, Dave Watson and Kevin Keegan could count themselves as anything like regulars. It seemed we would not qualify for the World Cup.

Here was a man who never shirked a match or a confrontation with Leeds United, suddenly ducking out of the one thing that was most important to the country – the England manager's job.

There were four real candidates for Revie's job – Ron Greenwood, Brian Clough, Bobby Robson and Lawrie McMenemy. I looked at the four, considered all their qualities and decided that as far as I was concerned Lawrie McMenemy was the man for the position. There may have been a selfish side to my thinking. I felt he would be good for me. I knew him well, liked the way he talked about the game and was impressed with the way he went about his business. He always seemed a solid, sensible, reliable type to me. Bobby Robson was not far behind for the same reasons, but I was unsure about Clough and Greenwood.

I knew there would be a lot of popular support for Clough. His record as a club manager was excellent, but so had Revie's been. Clough was his own man. He is not altogether the diplomat an international manager needs to be and I had a feeling he might have upset too many people in the past. Greenwood I associated with West Ham, a club who had always been a soft touch for Liverpool. He had stepped down as manager and handed over to John Lyall, so I could not see his credentials making him anything like an obvious choice for the job.

Obviously people at the FA knew a lot more about Ron Greenwood than I did. I was soon to learn of his qualities, for one of his first actions was to come to meet the Liverpool players.

We were playing at Middlesbrough and he arrived at the hotel. He wanted to meet the Englishmen – internationals past, present and prospective – and about eight of us went into a room with him.

He said, 'Right, I want you lads to tell me what you think of me as an England manager.'

It wasn't easy. We all had our thoughts, but to lay them on the line at this juncture seemed a risky business. He could sense our unease and opened the conversation a bit further by saying, 'Let me put it another way. I've come here to tell you that I intend to build my England squad around you.'

That gave us some leeway for conversation and with Ian Callaghan and myself doing most of the talking (as usual) I think we let him know pretty clearly that we felt he was a blackboard manager. A theorist with plenty of high blown ideas. At Liverpool, of course, simplicity is the watchword. To every one of us, theorists were people to be suspected.

He said, 'Let me assure you you couldn't be further from the truth. I train with players. I work with them. I don't fill their heads full of fancy talk. I try to talk in footballers' language.'

He talked sound sense to us. He was changing my view of him and I knew others were being influenced in the right way, too. Everything he said has since been borne out completely. We don't spend our time theorizing. We do it out on the field.

England's chances of qualifying for the 1978 World Cup had already been virtually blown, although that defiant match against Italy at Wembley which England won 2–0 really put everyone on to Greenwood's bandwagon. People liked his style. England played well. At last there was some hope in the air.

During much of the 1978–9 season I was injured and spent a long time out of the Liverpool side, but Ron Greenwood kept in touch with me.

I played in England's 4–0 win over Northern Ireland in February in the 1979 European Championship qualifying match, but again I was injured and out of the Liverpool first team as the home internationals and the summer tour squads were due to be announced.

The newspapers were full of speculation. Rumours had me going here, there and everywhere as manager, player-manager or just player. They all seemed to think my Liverpool days were over.

I was at home one day when Ron Greenwood telephoned. He said, 'Emlyn, what's happening?'

I told him, 'I've had a bad injury, but in the last three weeks I've played four reserve team games and feel better now than at any time in the last six months. I feel absolutely great.'

He said, 'That's good enough for me. Report for the home internationals.'

He told me he would probably be playing Phil Thompson in the side and I said that was fair enough, he did not need to explain anything to me and I felt that just being in the squad was a bonus.

Early in the week of the home internationals he came to me and said, 'I'm not saying that the match against

Wales will be your last for England, but I am making you skipper, and there's a chance that it could be your last. But what a nice way to go, as captain in front of your own crowd.'

It was lovely of him to put it that way. I thanked him, and then I went to my room determined that it would not be my last match. I was not ready to pack up. I wanted more England appearances. Pulling on the white shirt was something like an addiction with me.

I went out and played tremendously. I knew I had to. I was fighting to stay in the side.

As we walked off the field at the end of the o–o draw he caught up with me, put his arm round my shoulder and said, 'You're going to make it extremely difficult for me to leave you out, pal!'

Those were the words I wanted to hear. We went off on tour to Bulgaria, Sweden and Austria and he played me in Stockholm. I had another excellent match. I was delighted to have the chance to lend my experience in other directions, too.

The senior member of the international committee, Dick Wragg, paid me a glowing compliment when he said that he would suggest that even if I were not picked for a future squad I should be asked along to train with the players. He regarded my experience highly, and I think he thought I might be going out of the First Division.

We all have great faith and respect for Ron Greenwood as the man in charge of England's destiny. He has a quiet strength about him. He believes totally in his players. He talks common sense and his study of continental football has brought him a knowledge of the game that's unsurpassed.

He treats us like men, too. When we report for England get-togethers he allows us to have a pint if we want and simply says, 'Do as you please, but the hard work starts in the morning.'

Curfews are unwritten. No one abuses the freedom. I may go to bed at 9.30 pm, Kevin Keegan may stay up until midnight. We do what we are normally used to doing.

I enjoy working with Greenwood, in fact I've loved every moment of my England career, though I've had my share of criticism. I know I have never been a Bobby Moore or a Bobby Charlton but I have played under four England managers (they must rate among the best in the game to get that job) and I have been captain under three of them.

In ten years as an international I have been to parts of the world most people will see only on film and in books. I never ever imagined that the road out of Barrow-in-Furness would take me so far.

10

The Great Ones

I WAS LYING ON MY BED IN A HOTEL IN WOLVER-hampton with an ice pack on my left knee and a metal weight attached to my foot. It was a kind of home-treatment routine: the ice to help bring down the swelling and the weight to make sure that my muscles stayed in shape. It was a boring business, so I reached out for an old envelope and a pen and began doodling.

For something to do I decided to pencil in my greatest ever Liverpool team or, more accurately I suppose, the ten players I would love to play alongside as an eleven. Down the years so many great and good players have passed through the Anfield corridors that it turned out to be an immensely difficult task. I soon realized that I could choose three or four completely different elevens all capable of going out and winning the First Division Championship.

Eventually I came up with a team to play in 4-3-3 formation: Clemence, Lawler, Ron Yeats, myself, Gerry Byrne; Kevin Keegan, Ian St John, Peter Thompson; John Toshack, Kenny Dalglish and Roger Hunt. I have also chosen reserves to stand in for most of them because the choice I made left me having a number of arguments with myself.

Take the goalkeepers. The only two I've played with on a regular basis have been Ray Clemence and Tommy Lawrence, who was his predecessor. Choosing between them was not as easy as most people might think. Although Ray is, in my mind, the best goalkeeper in England since Gordon Banks in his prime, it must not be forgotten that Tommy Lawrence's contribution to the success of Liverpool was every bit as important as Ray's. I would agree that Tommy was not as good a save-maker as Ray, nor was he as imaginative in his distribution. But Tommy was one of the first goalkeepers to be used almost as an extra sweeper behind the defence and I know that Ray learned a lot from him.

But the place goes to Clem because he is such a gifted, natural athlete. Sometimes he staggers me with his laziness in training. He reports with the rest of the Liverpool lads and if he feels like it he will join in the five-a-side matches and so on. Or, depending on his whim, he may spend the morning just wandering around. There are several 'manufactured' goalkeepers around; people like Joe Corrigan of Manchester City. He is an excellent keeper, but one who has to work constantly at every facet of the art to maintain his standards. Clem seems not to need to work at anything. He is perfectly built for the job and is extremely athletic and quick. The only time I see him working hard is when he is away with England, and that is probably five or six times a year.

At right-back I've plumped for Chris Lawler, which may surprise a few people because the current Liverpool right-back, Phil Neal, is a regular England international.

I always felt that Chris was a vastly underrated player. He won all the honours with Liverpool, was never given a chasing by an opposing winger and managed to score a phenomenal fifty goals from the right-back position, yet he was never the team's penalty taker.

Chris, the original quiet man of football, used to sneak up on opponents in unbelievable positions for his goals – positions that surprised even his team-mates. We could be defending our own left-back position and then suddenly break away to cross the ball to the far post and frequently Chris would be ghosting in to head a crucial goal. Phil Neal is quick and smart and a lovely player, but after giving it a lot of thought I have to settle for Chris in the No. 2 shirt.

I have put myself in at centre-back because that is where I spent most of my Liverpool career. But who do I want alongside me? Is it Ron Yeats or Phil Thompson or Tommy Smith?

They all have their own special qualities. In the end I have to stay with my memories of that giant of a man, Ron Yeats. I was a mere kid when I first met him and I learned so much from him, especially about being a professional competitor. He was a huge, strong man who terrified opponents. He was part of the Liverpool foundations and an inspiration to everyone. I recall games where I was pleased with myself. I thought I was doing well, but there was no praise from Big Ron while we were on the field – just a rocket to keep me on my toes.

Only one man ever stood up to him and that was Joe Baker, the old Nottingham Forest centre-forward. Joe was never renowned as a brave player but he came from the same part of the world as Big Ron and whenever they met native pride was at stake. You could see it in their bruises afterwards.

Sadly, I have no room for Phil Thompson in my side. It is a pity because we played together in central defence when neither of us was a recognized centre-half. Teams were usually equipped with a bulky, stopper centre-half and a man to play off him. We were similar types and I like to think that we brought a new dimension to defensive techniques. We started by being thrown together and not knowing how things would work out. It could not have gone better. We played some marvellous matches and I can recall games when we never gave the opposition a kick. Whereas Yeats and Tommy Smith used to go in and battle for the ball before humping it upfield, we were happy to drop off and pass the ball around to each other and in that way could play ourselves out of trouble. Neither of us were embarrassed in possession, where the big fellow might have been.

It's also a shame that Tommy Smith must go into the reserve slot in my greatest of all Liverpool teams because, without doubt, he is the greatest captain I have ever played under. Although I never particularly got along with him as a man, I had nothing but admiration and respect for him as a captain on the pitch.

He had powerful qualities of leadership. He had always had to fend for himself as a youngster in Liverpool and it showed in his adult attitudes. He was hard. He was as ferocious with his own mates as he was with opponents. If he was having a bad time himself, it never affected his attitude to others. He kept battling away and shouting his orders. I'm afraid that I tend to clam up and say nothing when my own form is not so good.

Filling the left-back position was probably the hardest of all. Several players have filled the No. 3 shirt and played well but it does not seem to have been an enduring position. In the end I have to go for Gerry Byrne, another member of the great team that lifted Liverpool off the ground. I did not play with him a lot because he was coming to the end of his career when I moved to Liverpool from Blackpool. But whenever I heard Bill Shankly talk about Gerry there was a note of awe and admiration in his voice. They were always tales of bravery, of how the silent Gerry was so full of commitment that most visiting right-wingers used to go wandering to get away from him.

The 1965 FA Cup final provides the story that says everything about Gerry Byrne. In the third minute of Liverpool's match with Leeds United Gerry broke his collar-bone in a tackle with Bobby Collins. This was before the age of substitutes. Bob Paisley, who was Liverpool's trainer at the time, knew almost immediately what had happened. But Gerry played on, bravely disguising his agony and helped Liverpool to victory, 2–1, in extra time. Leeds never guessed Gerry's problem and had they known they would surely have tried to exploit it.

As Bill Shankly said at the time, 'Gerry's bones were grinding together, but he stuck it out and should have had all the medals himself.'

Amazingly, Gerry is one of shyest, most modest men you could ever wish to meet. In conversation the words have almost to be forced out of him.

Pushing Gerry for the No. 3 shirt in my side is a man who could do anything with the ball, but was too easy-going for his own good – Alec Lindsay. His left foot could talk. You could play the ball to him and his left foot could whip out the stitching and lace it back up again without you knowing. If I had Alec's skill to go with my enthusiasm

I could have been a truly extraordinary player. I played more than sixty times for England, many of those appearances at left-back, and yet I was never blessed with Alec's high level of skill.

He was a lazy character and but for that unfortunate trait I am sure he would still be playing in the First Division instead of running a fish-and-chip shop in Bury.

Choosing three men for midfield was a task that seemed almost impossible when I jotted down the list of contenders. I chose Kevin Keegan, Ian St John and Peter Thompson, but would not have quarrelled too harshly with anyone who offered Ian Callaghan, Gordon Milne and Ray Kennedy instead. Those three, of course, move into my shadow team.

I can imagine a few eyebrows being raised at the nomination of Peter Thompson for the left-hand side of midfield. But I always recall something that Shanks, in all his wisdom, once said: 'If ever you find that you're under pressure then give the ball to Peter Thompson because then you'll all be able to take a five-minute breather.'

Peter was blessed with all the talents. He could do anything with the ball. Occasionally his final pass or shot would go adrift and there were times when his play suggested that he might not be the brainiest player in the game. But he could beat people so easily. He could hold the ball for any length of time and few defenders could go and take it from him.

He was a lovely, quiet fellow, at his happiest on trips with his head in a novel. He let his feet do all the talking and they spelled out one awful message for the former England and Fulham full-back George Cohen.

He had just come back from a long spell out with injury. The Craven Cottage fans were delighted to see him back. He was a favourite of the trendy crowd down by the River

Thames and had, after all, played an important rôle in England's victorious World Cup in 1966.

Unfortunately, he cannot have been fully ready to meet the Peter Thompson trickery. Poor George was twisted this way and that as he tried to keep tabs on Peter. We won 2–0 and George Cohen was never an effective player again.

Ray Kennedy is pushing for that spot on the left of midfield. He is one player of whom you can be certain of scoring a goal in a certain situation. He used to be a forward, of course, and times his runs from the deep with perfection. He comes in late and does extremely well in knocking the ball down for other players to take advantage. Ray is an unspectacular, unfussy player and it was only when injury took him out of the team early in the 1979–80 season that the Anfield crowd began to appreciate his value to the team.

On the right-hand side of the field I take Kevin Keegan in front of Ian Callaghan. When Kevin was with Liverpool he was, without argument, the best player in British football. I exclude his last season at Anfield because I know he wanted to get away. His mind was elsewhere and no one can blame him for that.

In the years before he had been truly magnificent. He was the superb, all-round professional whose consistency was incredible. Much of that time, of course, he was a front player alongside John Toshack and their partnership gave everyone who followed Liverpool hour upon hour of pleasure. At the time they needed each other and Tosh certainly helped Kevin to make his name. I have choosen him in midfield because I now believe he is a better player when he is running on to things late from deeper midfield positions. It is a rôle he has filled so expertly for England in vital matches in recent seasons.

Off the field Kevin in one of my favourite people. He's an ideal team man. I've watched him closely throughout the seasons and although he is extremely bright he has such a happy-go-lucky, infectious, slapstick approach to life that he became known in the Liverpool dressing-room as Andy MacDaft.

One of his favourite tricks was to come into the dressing-room first thing in the morning clucking like a hen. And he would not stop. There was no conversation; just this infernal squawking which sounded like a hen that had laid an egg. He was a very generous fellow and I know that if ever I felt I needed to talk over a problem he would come to see me on the first available plane out of Hamburg.

Cally remains a living legend on Merseyside, even though he has joined John Toshack at Swansea City. Everything that Liverpool did and won under Bill Shankly and Bob Paisley, Ian Callaghan seems to have had a part in it. A measure of the consistently high standards he has set can be gauged from the fact that eleven years separated his first international cap from his second. During all those years from 1966 to 1977 he was always on the fringe of inter-national selection. He is an immensely likeable lad with no enemies. He never has a bad word to say about anyone.

He staggered us with an opinion at a team meeting on one occasion when we were due to meet Leeds. Battles between the clubs were renowned throughout the game. It was all that cock o' the north business. Before this particular match Shanks was running through the Leeds team and he came to Allan Clarke. Now, excellent player though Clarke might have been, and there was no disputing that he was an outstanding goal-scorer, he had a nasty streak or two. He was poker-faced, he moaned at referees and he wasn't averse to giving anyone a sly dig behind the referee's back.

Anyway Shanks dismissed Clarke quickly, saying, 'Allan Clarke, well, you all know about him.'

Suddenly from the back of the room Cally's voice piped

up, 'I don't like him.' That was all. No more, he had stated his feelings.

Everyone turned round. We couldn't believe it. Such a statement was so out of character. Someone said, 'Good heavens, Cally, you must be getting old if you're starting to slang people!'

In the middle of the three I have to go for the man who is probably revered above all on Merseyside – the Saint, Ian St John. Here was a brilliant, stealthy footballer in true Scottish mould. I learned so much from him that I feel I will always be in his debt. When I first went to Liverpool he was playing up front and his talent burned like a beacon, but even I never realized just how formidable his strengths were until he dropped back into midfield. There I was playing alongside him. His will to win never diminished. He was constantly talking, encouraging, and he had a gift of playing ground passes through little gaps alongside defenders as they ran out. It was a perfect ploy for our forwards to exploit. I would have loved to have been able to execute that kind of pass with the certainty Ian St John managed. When I look at the influence the Saint, and his pal Ronnie Yeats, had on my upbringing as a footballer I'm glad I was involved in the right set-up.

Not far behind the Saint, but far enough to be in my shadow squad, comes Gordon Milne. He was a dapper, one-touch player and because I was bought essentially to replace Gordon we did not play in the same side very often. But Shanks never tired of telling stories about Gordon Milne and one statement that stayed with me went like this: 'If you do half the job that Gordon Milne has done for me these last six or seven seasons then I'll be more than satisfied.'

That shows what Shanks thought of him. I was employed in a similar rôle during my early months and if I did, as

Shanks hoped, half a job then Gordon Milne must have been a superb player.

How much, I wonder, would my front three cost in today's market-place? John Toshack, Kenny Dalglish and Roger Hunt represent three of the most formidable front players I've ever seen. Thank goodness they were on my side, though occasionally I had to stand the torment of Toshack, who was Welsh, and the Scotsman Dalglish in international matches.

Then, thankfully, they were isolated. Already I can hear people muttering that Toshack was not so clever on the ground. That's completely false. He was certainly powerful in the air and while he would be the first to admit that his close control on the ground could have been better, he was intelligent enough to be able to drift around taking opponents out of the way and allowing plenty of space for better ball-players to operate.

A classic example of this occurred in a match against Chelsea at Stamford Bridge. In the pre-match publicity Chelsea's big centre-half Micky Droy had been boasting that he wasn't worried about Toshack's presence. He could take care of Tosh. As it happened we won 1–0 and Tosh had dragged Micky to almost every corner of the pitch, leaving Kevin Keegan to fizz and explode in the huge gap that was left down the middle.

As we were leaving the field at the end I went up to congratulate Tosh. I knew exactly what he had done for the team that day. He had not been spectacular but he had been unselfish. His value to the team had been enormous.

We were heading towards the tunnel together when Micky Droy ran across, dug Toshack in the side and said, 'Never gave you a kick today.'

Tosh looked at me, shook his head and said, 'Yeah, you never gave me a kick. You marked me at left-back. You marked me at outside-right and you marked me at right-half.'

'Yeah,' said Micky. 'Did well, didn't I?'

Tosh tried again. 'Where were you when Kevin went nipping through for the goal?' he asked.

'I was marking you,' said Droy.

End of conversation.

Imagine the scoring potential of Toshack working alongside Dalglish. It was not to be. By the time Kenny had joined Liverpool as Kevin Keegan's replacement Tosh's legs were giving him trouble and he was on his way to player-management elsewhere. They played together only once, in Liverpool's 5–1 win over Dinamo Dresden, and that match was the perfect illustration of the strength of their weaponry.

Kenny is very much like Kevin. They are both quick to snap up chances. Their brainwork is incisive and decisive. Kenny at the moment is unquestionably the best player in British football. I love to see him play. He is almost impossible to mark.

With him and Tosh in my front line I have Roger Hunt. He was bold and honest and had a powerful shot. The fans loved him because he was silent and strong and he could play the game with never a bad thought in his head.

What a front three, with Tosh knocking the balls down, Roger running on to them and Dalglish jinking his way into all sorts of positions past defenders. They were so good that I'm not going to name three players to stand by, ready to take their places in my shadow side. John Toshack, Roger Hunt and Kenny Dalglish, the Welshman, the Englishman and the Scotsman, stand alone. And always will.

11

The Dream Comes True

THROUGHOUT ALL THE HEADY PROGRESS MADE BY Liverpool Football Club, through championships and FA Cups and UEFA Cups which came to decorate the Anfield sideboard, one trophy remained out of reach.

The European Cup became the ultimate goal. This is the trophy played for by the champion clubs of all the countries in Europe. Even to get into the hat for the first-round draw meant that we had to win the First Division Championship. Liverpool were champions in 1976 and so, once again, we were on the trail of the big silver urn. Winning that trophy would strike a blow for British football because at international level we had not been doing too well.

We had an unusual send-off as we left for Rome for the

1977 European Cup final against Borussia Moenchenglad-bach. We had been beaten 2–1 by Manchester United in the FA Cup at Wembley; hardly the sort of result to put singing optimism in our hearts. The build-up to Rome began in that Wembley dressing-room right after the match.

We were disappointed. We had not played well and no one needed telling. Long faces stared at the floor. Champagne remained unopened and Bob Paisley, Joe Fagan and Ronnie Moran moved about quietly.

What was there to say? It was no time for recriminations and nobody felt like turning to his neighbour to say 'Sorry'. We had lost when we would have beaten Manchester United nine times out of ten. Suddenly all the miserable silence was broken by the man who is probably the worst loser of all, goalkeeper Ray Clemence. He took a grip of the situation, stalked over to the champagne, lifted a bottle out and aimed an exploding cork at the high ceiling. Then he said with clinical determination, 'To hell with all this. I'm going to get pissed. We've got Wednesday to come.'

And so we had. There was no need to be moping. Ray's gesture lifted the cloud. We all had a drink and the train that took us straight back to Merseyside was one long mobile party. A stranger climbing aboard would have thought we had won the Cup. We were all back to normal; the FA Cup final forgotten as the European final loomed.

Normality meant that Liverpool would treat that game no differently from any other. The trip to Italy was just another mission. Most of us had lost count of how many times we had been abroad for vital matches, so why should we get unduly excited about this one? There was no fancy talk from us. None of the players spoke in terms glorifying the match. There was no bragging. If anything the match was deliberately played down because the last thing we needed was additional pressure being put on anyone. That attitude has been inherited down the years and I hope that I may have helped to pass some of it on so that the next generation of Liverpool players will benefit.

Some clubs make such tournaments a special event. They pile on the pressure and make it too important by transporting the wives on the same plane. A holiday spirit catches on and the serious thinkers are distracted by peripheral things. It isn't possible to avoid the glare of extra publicity altogether and when we trained on the morning of the match there were more spectators than many Third and Fourth Division clubs in England attract on match days.

Some of the tension slipped through then, but all that was waived as we set off from our hotel on the outskirts of the city for the ground. The streets were alive with red and white. The Scousers had taken over. Their banners were everywhere. They were full of optimism. They had flooded Rome, arriving by plane, train, car and good old-fashioned hitch-hiking. They kicked up so much noise that the final, played in the magnificent stadium that was the scene of the 1960 Olympic Games, was something like a home match.

We played well. Everything was running for us and when Terry McDermott put us in front I could see myself going up to collect the Cup. Such thoughts are dangerous. Alan Simonsen, the little Dane who was a gifted and inventive player, put the Germans level and they responded with a purple patch in which only the agility of Ray Clemence kept us in the game. We could have been dead and buried.

But something else was going on out there on the pitch. Kevin Keegan was not only playing his heart out for Liverpool, he was trying to sell himself to the many foreign clubs who had their representatives up in the stands. All season there had been talk of his moving abroad. Real Madrid had been mentioned and Barcelona along with the Italians of Juventus. They had all sent their men to watch Kevin in the First Division but no bids had been forthcoming. Now he had centre stage ... the European Cup final.

Eight months earlier Kevin had been captain of the England side that had been defeated in the World Cup qualifying match; the game that had marked my own international comeback under Don Revie. That had been a depressing night, for the result really spelled the end of England's World Cup interest.

This was different. The Germans decided that Bertie Vogts, the fine little defender who was to take over from Franz Beckenbauer as his country's captain, should play a tight-marking game on Kevin. Vogts never had a chance. Kevin was in irresistible form. After Tommy Smith had given us a 2–1 lead Vogts's frustration spilled over. He had been turned inside out by Kevin's determined and elusive running and finally the lunging tackle of a beaten desperado gave us a penalty and Phil Neal stroked the ball home to put victory beyond Moenchengladbach's reach. Europe saw some of Liverpool's finest football that night ... and some of Kevin's.

Moenchengladbach were so impressed with the way he demoralized his marker that they immediately tried to sign him. But Kevin had already come to terms with sv Hamburg. I was sorry to see him go, but I knew that he would succeed and to benefit oneself is a right to which every man must hold.

Anyway, we had done it. The great Cup was ours. The night was alive with the joyous celebrations of the Liverpool supporters. If ever a picture told the story of my own sheer, unbridled joy, it is the one of me lifting the trophy aloft.

And yet when I was climbing the stairs to receive the Cup

I was not thinking about Kevin Keegan, or myself, or the match we had just dominated so comprehensively. Through my mind flashed several old familiar faces ... Tommy Lawrence, Ron Yeats, Shanks, Reuben Bennett, Eric Roberts, a former chairman, Sid Reakes, a director, and the old President, T. V. Williams. I knew as I went to reach out to take the European Cup that I was just a collector for all of them.

This was the moment for which they had slaved for over fourteen hard years. Some of them were no longer with Liverpool. That did not matter; I knew it would be enough for them to see that their wild dream, born so many years ago, had finally come true.

Like everything Liverpool have ever set out to do, the celebrations matched the occasion. In every way, on and off the field, Liverpool have been setting standards for the others to follow.

Walking into the hotel was like walking on to the Kop. The fans were there in their thousands. How they managed it I will never know. They had been at the game, of course, and while we had a police escort through the crowded streets back to the hotel the fans had managed to beat us.

They all wanted to touch the Cup. They sang and danced. And we knew, as we walked into the most impressive buffet I have ever seen, that money would be no object in a party that was to go on all night long. A table groaning with turkeys, suckling pig, game, salmon and the rest stretched for thirty yards down the middle of the room. A nod of the head brought waiters running with bottles of champagne or cases of lager. Some of the lads still preferred lager.

We helped ourselves to food and sat around the tables. I was with Barbara, who had joined us with the rest of the wives after the match, and we sat with John Toshack and his wife Sue. I felt for Tosh. He had missed the final because of injury. He had been a part of things for so long and had worked feverishly in the hope of getting fit. But he knew – we all knew – that he had little chance of making it.

I watched him eating his food quietly. I could only guess how he must have been feeling. He would be delighted for the lads, but thoroughly miserable in himself because he would feel that he had no part in it. I would have been dejected. I looked at the Cup towering over the food and knew I had to keep my medal in my pocket.

I wanted to pull it out and look at it. I wanted to show it to Tosh, but I knew that this was not the time.

The party began sedately enough. There were the players, officials and the invited journalists. A strong-arm Italian was on the door to keep out gate-crashers, but he was no match for the Liverpool supporters. They swarmed in and joined us. They drank what they could and finished off the buffet. They had their photographs taken with the Cup and there wasn't a moment's trouble.

In some respects they made the party go with an extra swing. There has always been a strong bond between the Liverpool team and the supporters – a feeling encouraged by Shanks. But I was glad not to be picking up the tab, for people were still clutching champagne bottles round the swimming-pool when the sun came up!

Tosh got over his depression pretty quickly and as we winged our way home on another champagne special he was the life and soul of the party with his mimicry. His impersonation of Johan Cruyff over the airplane address system was so perfect that some people wondered if the Dutchman was indeed on board.

As holders, there was only one thing to do. We had to go out and win the European Cup for the second year in succession, which was something no other British team had achieved. It was not our best year in the First Division, for we finished second, seven points behind Nottingham Forest who had a glorious season responding to the driving style of management of Brian Clough and Peter Taylor.

But in Europe we were invincible. It seemed that the continentals were terrified of us. They remembered how we had played in Rome and they had heard all the stories of how we played seventy matches in a season. People expected us to win the European Cup again and we expected to win it ourselves. Dinamo Dresden (East Germany) were swept aside, then the Portuguese of Benfica failed to give us a test, but the biggest disappointment of all was the semi-final against Borussia Moenchengladbach, our old friends from the previous year's final. They beat us 2–1 in West Germany in the first leg but then completely folded when Ray Kennedy scored an early goal back at Anfield.

Like everyone else we played they sat on defence and Kenny Dalglish and Jimmy Case gave us a comfortable passage to the final at Wembley. That continued in the mood of anti-climax. Bruges seemed beaten before they started. We were not at our best. I suppose we had the experience to do just what was needed. Kenny Dalglish scored the goal that gave us the trophy for the second year in succession but we were somehow not bursting with the pride we had felt in Rome.

Bruges were a disgrace. It seemed to me they were playing for a goalless draw, hoping in their wild despair that the match might eventually be decided on penalties. What an attitude to take into a European Cup final.

12

Another Business

JOHN TOSHACK ... A RARE CHARACTER. A WELSH-man with that nation's flair for words. We were great pals at Liverpool and for a spell we shared a sports shop business in Formby. It was a laugh-a-minute existence dealing with the Scousers. They all wanted a bargain. They all wanted to talk football with that mixture of knowledge and humour that separates Merseyside from the rest of the football world.

John could spot a con-man a mile away. I was more gullible. The hard cases usually got the better of me.

In the early days of the business we used to travel around Merseyside in the evenings attending meetings of the various local leagues. We had decided that such personal selling techniques would help us provide kits for the junior players of the region.

They would be meeting to discuss the state of pitches, players who had been disciplined and teams whose strips and personnel were sub-standard. They all knew we were there for business reasons but when you are a junior league official and there are two Liverpool first-teamers on your doorstep you ask them in and make them welcome.

Tosh usually did the talking. He would tell them that whatever they were paying for their football gear we felt sure we could give them a better deal. Quite a few of them went along with us and regularly they provided us with the same problem.

Take the fellow in Wavertree. He sent us his £10 deposit for his £50 set of shirts and fourteen days later they arrived at the shop made up. He told us he had the money so we decided to deliver the goods.

'Morning,' said Tosh. 'Brought the kit. Got the money have you then?'

'Ah well, you see, Tosh, it's like this . . .' the Scouser began, and straight away we knew we were in trouble. 'We've got the money all right, but the missus is keeping it in her purse, safe like, and she's gone out.'

At that point I would have handed over the kit and told the man to let us have the money when his wife returned. I was hopeless when the time came to be hard with people.

But Tosh just said, 'Right, when your missus comes back give us a ring and we'll bring the stuff back again.'

Then the Scouser groaned, 'But, Tosh, we need the strip for tomorrow. We've got an important match, honest.'

Again I would have parted, but Tosh came straight back and said, 'Aye, and we need the money.'

That was typical of the cases we were dealing with every week. Working with Tosh opened my eyes. I don't suppose

I'll be able to spot every con-man I come across in my life, but he made me aware of people's craftiness and I hope I may have learned something for when I eventually go into football management.

If I enjoyed that experience, it was nothing compared to the fun and the thrills I have had in my one indulgence – National Hunt racing.

Ever since those early boyhood days at Cartmel when my father used to run his book on 'Ginger's Hill' I've been fascinated by the mechanics of horse-racing. The people interest me and the horse is a beautiful, brave and intelligent animal.

The thought of actually being an owner never occurred to me until I joined Liverpool. I regarded owners as lords and ladies and the gentry of the country. But one day Peter Thompson introduced me to his friend Bernard Bargh, with whom he was in partnership in a garage opposite the Liverpool ground. It is now run by another former Liverpool player, Gordon Wallace, incidentally. We started talking horses and it turned out that Bernard had a friend who knew the north-country trainer Peter Easterby, one of the finest trainers in the country. They could see how interested I was and suggested I went in with them. I took a sixth share in a horse called Privy Star. The down payment was £125 and after that the feeding and training costs were £10 a week. It was all good fun and I had my first experience of race-horse ownership.

Again there was no romantic sequel. Privy Star was no Nijinsky. More of a Dobbin, really, because she ran two dozen times and never once managed the frame. But it wasn't expensive, and I had just started to earn good money at Liverpool and had no responsibilities. I used to go and watch the horse struggle round at Haydock and Catterick and courses that were not too difficult to reach after training.

Privy Star had to go, however, and in her place we had a horse recommended to us by Easterby. It was called La Cilla and this time we were on to something good. The horse ran five times, won on three occasions and was placed in the other two. We had bought her for 2,400 guineas and sold for 5,200 guineas, so we showed a handsome profit.

I dropped out of racing then and watched with interest from a distance, until I moved to my present house in Formby, just down the road from the famous Red Rum stables of Don 'Ginger' McCain. I had met him before and now we became firm friends. He is a marvellously knowledgeable trainer but because his yard is not in one of the more fashionable racing areas he doesn't always attract the best horses. Red Rum, of course, remains the wonder of his stables. His sensational victories in the Grand National, the toughest steeplechase of all, have made him a national character and now 'Rummy' spends his days opening fêtes and parading in carnivals, but you can still find him bucking and pulling on the early-morning gallops on the beach where Don McCain prepares his charges so well.

I have had three or four moderate performers with Don on and off over the last few seasons and he came to me late in 1978 with a proposition I could not refuse. It was my testimonial and Don, who was on my committee, said that he didn't think he was doing enough to help. In fact he was attending many of my dinners and I knew that his name on the guest list would bring in a lot of punters, which meant that I was quite happy with everything he was doing.

Anyway, he said that he had bought a horse from Ladbroke's chairman Cyril Stein and that it was qualified for the 1978 and 1979 Grand Nationals. He said that if I took it over it could turn out to be an excellent publicity vehicle for my testimonial year and that Ladbroke's would be interested in my progress and that of the horse, Wayward Scot.

As it happened, Ladbroke's made a donation to my pool and named a race after me at the Grand National meeting, so it was soon turning out to be one of the best ideas I had ever known.

Scottie, as we called him, was never going to win the National. He experienced some leg trouble and had not run for eighteen months when the big race was looming. He was a rank outsider, for there were many better performers in the field.

We gave him two warm-up races and these showed his form figures immediately before the National of third and fourth. Those who follow racing closely will know that there were only three and four runners in the races! He failed to get round Aintree but he more than paid for himself in terms of publicity for my testimonial.

Scottie had a surprise for us, though. Don decided to run him on the last day of the jumping season at Uttoxeter. The horse had been working well and Don fancied him so much that he engaged the top jockey, Jonjo O'Neill, to ride him. I was tingling with excitement at the thought of leading in a winner. I had my bet worked out and the day couldn't come quickly enough. It's only occasionally I have a flutter, by the way.

Drama came on the eve of the meeting, however, with Jonjo damaging a shoulder and being unfit to ride. Don called up Ron Barry, a former champion jockey, so the horse was still in expert hands. Scottie was full of himself, looking brighter than I had ever seen him before.

At the track Don and I met Ron Barry and we all went for a cup of tea before the race. We discussed prospects and the way Scottie likes to run and then Ron said, 'Whatever you're planning to put on him, halve it.'

It transpired that Ron had ridden the favourite, Sea Urchin, on a track in the north-east the previous week. He

said Sea Urchin was a better horse and although it had not
been fully wound up to win that day they were really having
a go here. I took his advice and halved my gamble.

Off he went to get changed and we saw him into the
saddle and out of the paddock before we climbed up to
the stand. Our horse was leading all the way. At Uttoxeter
the horses come straight at you, head on, and as they
approached the third last flight I could see he was going
well. Don confirmed it. The excitement was growing. The
adrenalin was rushing. My binoculars were shaking in my
hands. Scottie was battling. His ears were stuck forward,
his head was thrusting out, but suddenly Don said darkly,
'He's going to get done. Sea Urchin is coming to do him.'

I could see the dreaded Sea Urchin looming ominously
alongside and they jumped the fence together. Suddenly
Ron gave Scottie a couple of reminders with his whip and
he buckled down to business so earnestly that he surged
ahead again and Sea Urchin's challenge was spent.

'He's going to win it!' cried Don and again my heart
soared, only to fall a little as another horse came to join
him at the last and Don was sighing, 'He's going to get done
on the line.'

As they approached the fence I could just see the tops
of the horses and the hard-working jockeys in the saddles.
Just before they took off Ron gave him three whacks down
his side, another two while he was in mid-air and two more
when they landed. The horse responded with courage and
charged on to win by a length and a half with me cheering
myself hoarse.

Don turned to me and said, 'He's won it, but we might
just lose it again in the stewards' room for rough riding.'

We survived, but Ron had made the horse work for his
victory. There was nothing cruel in the use of the whip;
it was a case of Scottie needing to be bundled along. Horses

are bright creatures and he knew every inch of the way what was happening and with those reminders from his pilot he stuck to his task.

I was overwhelmed with excitement. Although horses of mine had won before, this was the first time I had actually been at a meeting to see it happen. There will always be a soft spot in my heart for Wayward Scot. He was a marvellous servant to us. We paid a modest 800 guineas for him, kept him for a year, derived yards of publicity from him, ran him in the Grand National and had a good winning bet on him at 6–1. After all that we sold him for 3,000 guineas and put the profit into another prospective jumper who is in training but, as yet, is unnamed.

Racing is an interesting escape for me. The people who follow National Hunt racing are sporting, generous and good-humoured folk. They know what they are talking about. There is no humbug and they go to meetings to enjoy each others' company and the spectacle of seeing fine animals tackling obstacles they wouldn't face if they weren't brave, enthusiastic and extremely wise beasts.

13

Looking
Back

NOW THAT I'M IN THE AUTUMN OF MY CAREER I occasionally look back a decade or so and try to compare the game on a then-and-now level. I hope no one will think I'm getting sour if I say that things aren't as good as they were. I love the game still. I would play for nothing. Indeed if Wolves told me I was no longer required I'm sure I would find myself turning out for my brother's Sunday League team in Barrow-in-Furness, provided the old legs would stand it, of course!

I'm saddened that standards have been lowered. I recall years ago I used to look at the First Division table at the start of every season. It was a frightening prospect. I considered the teams and I knew that any one of them

– Manchester United, Everton, Arsenal, Leeds, Spurs, West Brom, Chelsea, Manchester City, Wolves and the rest – were all capable of winning the title. We knew, at Liverpool, that wherever we had to go to play we were in for a fierce time.

Today this is no longer the case. Just look at the teams and you must realize that some of the so-called biggest names in the business are never going to win a First Division title again. Too many of them are uniform, ordinary teams. Liverpool have been way out on their own in terms of technique for the past five or six years and the only club which has looked capable of taking them on are Nottingham Forest, and they've hit a poor patch in recent times. But can Forest show the consistency of Liverpool? And are Liverpool as strong as they were? The whole picture looks depressing to me.

Why? What have they lost, these clubs who used to fill their rivals with so much fear? If I were still a Liverpool player I would look around the First Division and regard two-thirds of the teams with something like contempt. I would feel they had nothing that could make me worry.

Perhaps the coaches have something to do with it. In their text-book mediocrity too many of them seem to have driven the character and characters out of the game. Everything is uniform. There are teams surviving because they are full of faceless men all doing their chores without flair, without individuality but with an apprehension that makes their sole aim that of preventing the other team from playing.

Ten years ago every team had its characters. Bold men who had the confidence to do things their own way. I'm talking of players such as Francis Lee, Rodney Marsh, Mike Summerbee, Denis Law, Jimmy Greaves, George Best, Alan Ball, Alex Young, Ian St John and Ronnie Yeats.

They were giants of their time. They weren't bugged by

negative thoughts. They just went out and did their thing. Not only were they outstanding performers but they could turn an entire afternoon into a theatrical experience for the supporters. There were whole teams that you could recite by heart because every man had his own individual strengths.

Nowadays the coaches have brought everyone down to a level that is detrimental to football. However, every so often a glittering talent will emerge. Kenny Dalglish, for instance, would have been a star in any era. The opposing coaches now tend to pick some negative dunderhead with orders to stop Kenny from playing.

They usually fail, but what would have happened ten years ago if the same coaches had decided to put someone on the park to mark George Best at Manchester United? They tried it, and then found United had others equally capable of taking them apart – Denis Law, Bobby Charlton, Nobby Stiles, Pat Crerand, Johnny Aston, Willie Morgan, David Sadler. There was always someone waiting to take up the challenge because Sir Matt Busby was one of those managers who encouraged his men to play attacking football. To be honest, I must own up to being able to see the decline in standards as applied to Wolves. Opponents try to bottle up Andy Gray and John Richards in the knowledge that we are unlikely to produce other players capable of ripping them apart.

Of course, at the moment in present-day football there are young professionals whose attitude isn't quite right. They are the ones who seem to feel that football owes them a living. They are the ones I'm sure Don Revie was talking about when he made one of his more heartening statements. He was talking to his Leeds players in their very early days when he said, 'You should go down on your knees every night before you go to bed and say thank you for being

allowed to be a member of such a privileged profession.'
Revie was from humble origins on Teesside and he never
forgot that.

Not very long ago there was an outcry from some
managers and referees about an outbreak of what they
called 'conning and cheating'. They were talking about
players trying to undermine the authority of referees, deliberate feigning of injury, diving to gain free-kick awards
and often behaving in a way that would lead to rivals being
sent off.

I'm not sure the game is any worse these days, but I am
certain that referees are under greater pressure than ever
before. A few years ago a wrong decision leading to a lost
point or even two might cost a player £30 in bonuses. Now
that figure has risen to as much as £200. The poor old
referee has only to make a mistake and everyone is ready
to knife him. By far the most sinister pressure comes from
the slow-motion replays on television. If he makes a mistake
it's replayed over and over again and, of course, we can
all reach the right verdict with the hindsight of a replay.
I'm not surprised that referees are nervous of the device.
In a match they have only a split second to make up their
minds. As far as I'm concerned we have some of the best
referees in the world. They are honest and brave and it's
wrong that week after week they should be subjects of trial
by television. I would ban the action-replay from being used
with regard to refereeing decisions.

There is one other modern aspect of this grand old game
that appals me and, I'm sure, the rest of my profession –
the bad language and behaviour on the terraces. It all
seemed to begin five or six years ago. Suddenly the teenage
gangs had taken over the terraces – not at the Liverpool
Kop, mind you, where the real hooligan of other grounds
would not be tolerated.

I look at my son Emlyn now in the same way I'm sure my father looked at me. I would love him to get as much pleasure as I have done out of sport. I would like to think that one day he might be a professional footballer because it's a grand life, full of excitement, travel and good living. If he could emulate everything I have done I would be more than delighted.

But I have to admit that the way things stand I would not let him go to a match on his own when he is older. Nor would I let him go with a gang of lads. The bad language is foul enough but as he gets older it's inevitable that he will learn what it all means. I am frightened for the safety of youngsters at football matches.

As he gets older he can come along with me to watch games if he wishes, but is it not terrible for a sporting father to have to admit that he would not let his lad go to a match alone because of the fear of his being hit on the head with a dart or a brick?

This, I'm afraid, is the great social problem that has attached itself to football and it's something that distresses all of us who care about the game.

When I was a youngster in Barrow there was never any trouble. I admit the crowds were rarely above four thousand people but we had our rivals. I don't recall supporters 'effing and blinding'. We had our chants and if the goalkeeper was rubbish we told him so. But we didn't feel the need to swear.

The Liverpool Kop were probably the innovators of mass chanting and singing, but they did it with humour and not filth. Inevitably their manners have declined with everyone else and it's so saddening.

14

The Last Salute

ALMOST THE FINAL ACT OF MY UNFORGETTABLE period at Liverpool involved my testimonial match and dinner which came at the end of a year of activity. There is no doubt that being involved in visiting pubs and clubs, and arranging dinners and other functions, took two years off my career as an Anfield player. Although the whole business has given me financial security for the rest of my life I would have regretted every moment and penny of it had I not walked into such instant success with Wolves.

Money is not everything and never has been with me. A career of football enjoyment was always my goal and I remain one of those people who, as long as they have a tenner with which to buy someone a drink, are happy.

Wolves, thankfully, quickly repaired the sadness I felt at having to leave Liverpool. I must be honest and say that when I first joined them in the summer of 1979 I thought Wolves would struggle. I was comparing everything and everyone with Liverpool. Then suddenly we were winning games. We were in the top half of the First Division and in the Football League Cup final against Nottingham Forest.

People often ask me what I have been able to give Wolves. I suppose I can call on the extra experience of playing in important matches. In decisive matches that put a strain on young players unused to the big occasion I can be the calming, controlling influence. I remember a moment in the League Cup quarter-final replay against Grimsby. We were leading 2–0 with five minutes to go and a ball was played down the line into our half. I guess ninety-nine players out of a hundred would have clobbered it away into touch. I shaped to head the ball, the Grimsby player who was chasing stood off and bought the dummy, and I gently chested the ball down for Derek Parkin to clear. Afterwards, Richie Barker, the Wolves assistant manager said, 'That is exactly what we bought you for.'

Similarly, in the semi-final against Swindon I was able to show friend and foe alike that I could take the pressure in my stride. We were 3–1 up and naturally they were hitting long passes forward to the respected attacking partnership of Andy Rowland and Andy Mayes, both prolific goal-scorers. I knew that whatever they tried I would win every ball. I had kept Rowland down for so long that, for all his elbowing and bustling, I knew I would stay on top. Again Barker told me, 'Through your experience in the last ten minutes you have made certain of getting us to Wembley.'

It was a lovely sentiment to drive home with and made that tiring testimonial year, when I seemed to be out every night and often tossed and turned in bed with worry, all seem worthwhile.

I have a feeling that football may have seen the last of the big testimonials. With freedom of contract virtually meaning freedom of movement it is less likely that players will stay at the same club for such lengthy spells. And the testimonial match itself has become something of an old chestnut.

Liverpool players have tried everything in the past. Serious games, farcical matches, gimmicks, five-a-side showbiz knockabouts, but what the public really wants to see is a serious competitive match. So we decided to be as serious as possible and invited along our old adversaries Borussia Moenchengladbach. We won 2–1 and I was thrilled by the fact that 26,500 people turned up at a time when Liverpool were involved in all the competitions and, consequently, causing a drain on everyone's pockets.

The testimonial year produced some marvellous moments and I treasure a letter the committee received from the Prime Minister, Mrs Margaret Thatcher. It read:

At the 1977 Cup final I remember the faces of the Liverpool players as they queued up to receive their losers' medals. Beneath their obvious disappointment at not being able to achieve the Treble I could see their minds were already turning to the European Cup game a few days later.

No player typifies this kind of determination and strength of character more than Emlyn Hughes. He has set a fine example as captain of Liverpool and with the help of the faithful Kop the Club has reached even greater heights under his captaincy and Bob Paisley's management.

It is fitting that Emlyn should have been granted a Testimonial and I would like to send my own personal good wishes for its success.

We are honouring a great sportsman and I am sure that the

response will underline the respect which people hold for Emlyn Hughes not only in Liverpool but well beyond the city boundaries.

There were other rewarding moments which will stay in my mind for the rest of my life. Not least among these was the willingness to help by people who are stars, and busy ones at that, in their own right. From every branch of sport and show business people came to support my dinners – Max Boyce, Henry Cooper, Jonjo O'Neill, Jimmy Tarbuck – I could count on them all as well as Liverpool's traditional rivals, Everton. Cliff Morgan even flew to Merseyside from the Continent to speak in his lovely, intimate, lilting style.

One of our star guests was the triple Grand National winner Red Rum. During the course of the meal the guests were introduced one by one until the MC came to the last table where 'Rummy's' trainer, Don McCain, was seated. He was introduced and the MC added: 'Don has a very special friend he would like you to meet.'

With that Don went to the double doors and brought in Red Rum himself. The old horse walked down the carpet between the tables and loved every minute of it. His ears were pricked. He gazed round the room. That horse is a star.

There were other stars of the year who are unknown outside their own circles of family and friends – Bob Moss, Terry Newell and Marvin Goldsmith. They were giants of humanity and kindness as they went about the business of organizing the testimonial that made me a much richer man. They never took a halfpenny, nor expected one. When people talk about the salt of the earth I know exactly what they mean. Bob, Terry and Marvin are in that league.

15

Crazy Horse OBE

I WAS HAVING A LIE-IN. JUST STARING AT THE ceiling, ruminating about the day ahead. It was a day off, although there were things to attend to. Letters, shopping, telephone calls to be made. Barbara was downstairs with the kids, Emlyn junior and Emma, and I heard the postman at the door. Nothing unusual in that, except that Barbara was suddenly taking the stairs two at a time. We often joke about her inquisitiveness whenever letters come addressed to me. She loves to look over my shoulder as if she is frightened of missing something.

Letters from the Football Association, inviting me to join an England squad, always give us a great kick but one look at the letter she carried on this particular morning explained her breathlessness. It was imposing. It was sealed with the red wax of a Government stamp.

'Emlyn, what have we got here? What have you done?' Barbara was firing the questions as though the letter contained some grave legal summons.

Curiosity was beginning to get the better of me, but I said calmly, 'Well, we won't know what's afoot until we open it.' I tore it open and together we must have read it half a dozen times. As I started to read my eyes somehow skipped a few lines and alighted upon the mention of the OBE – the Order of the British Empire. Would I accept the honour which the Queen of England was prepared to bestow on me?

It took some time for all this to sink in. I was to be included in the New Year's Honours list of 1980. The letter stressed that absolute secrecy must be maintained for there were still a few weeks to go before the official announcement would be made. Keeping that to myself was a very difficult task.

I suddenly felt terribly humble, and yet grateful to whoever had nominated me. There have been awards for football people before and I must be honest about one thing: I always felt deep down that if I was fair with everyone, if I played the game and never cheated and never got above myself then, with my playing success, there might just be something like an honour round the corner. But this was definitely something that was much more of a distant hope than an expectation.

Barbara was beside herself with delight. I was just overwhelmed. I read the letter. Put it down. And then read it again. This process went on over and over again.

In spite of the plea for secrecy, one very special person had to be told: my mother, up in Barrow-in-Furness. I knew she would be bursting with pride and, like me, would wonder how my father might have reacted had he still been alive. As I read the letter over again I could not help thinking about my father. It was he who inspired my respect for the Royal Family. Throughout our childhood we were always together in front of our little black-and-white television set listening to the Queen's Christmas broadcast. Nobody moved. Nobody whispered and my father used to hang on every word. And each year as the Queen's message ended he used to say the same thing. 'Great woman, that one.'

My mother, Anne to her friends, is also a queen in my reckoning. I have always been very close to her. When we were youngsters, my brothers David and Gareth and me, she always used to say that I was the sensible one. I think she may have changed her mind about that now.

Whenever I go home now my feet never seem to touch the ground. My brothers whisk me up to the working men's club and it seems there are old friends at every turn; all of them wanting to pump my hand. They are all like long lost brothers and as we ricochet from pillar to post I often hear my mother saying: 'How on earth I thought you were the sensible one I will never know.'

Mother is a serene, calming influence over the house. She was always the one with the biggest share of feet-on-the-ground common sense.

How well I remember those early winters when I was try-ing to make my way at Blackpool. I was just a kid and on those days when my father could not travel to see me play I used to hitch-hike home to Barrow for the weekend. I would set off after a fourth-team game usually with an empty stomach. The first part of the journey was not too difficult. There were always lorry drivers keen to have a passenger for company along the main A6 road that ran up the western side of England all the way to Scotland. But I had to turn left for Barrow at Levens Bridge with another thirty miles of road that was often dark and lonely. Sometimes I had to walk for fair stretches of this twisting, turning road but always one thought kept me going. 'I hope mother's got steak-and-kidney pie on,' I used to say to myself. Home and steak-and-kidney pie represented the warm and comforting oasis at the end of a long and hungry trek.

With my father such a dominant personality, mother was usually pushed into the background. But she was always there when I needed her. She never let anyone down. Her judgements were always sound.

I will never forget her reaction when a letter-writer in the local newspaper, the *North Western Evening Mail*, had a bit of a pop at me. I have always felt that the local paper seemed reluctant to give me a favourable mention and, strange though it may seem, recognition by your own folk is always especially rewarding. Anyway, the letter that appeared was very much below the belt.

Because it was my testimonial year at Liverpool I had taken some draw tickets to a few of the local pubs and clubs. They were just to be placed behind the bars and if anyone wanted a shot at the prizes, so much the better.

It seemed that one soul took exception to this. The letter-writer said that I had earned my money from football as a well-paid professional and that I should get out of the game gracefully. Why, he asked, should he be expected to buy tickets to support someone who had earned more from football than most Barrow people earn in a lifetime? I saw the letter and it hurt. I like to think that I have worked for everything. It was never easy living with the insecurity, the long hours of full-time work and part-time football and life in lodgings. Often I had nothing to eat all day and all the time lived with the knowledge that I was only as good as my last match – and some of the early ones were not very good at all – and that I could break a leg at any time. Of course I enjoyed the life because I was chasing a dream, but the letter seemed unusually vindictive to me.

Mother saw it of course and the reply that appeared a couple of days later definitely had her stamp on it. The writer argued that he or she had plenty of memories of Emlyn Hughes and they were all fond ones. It went on: 'It is not so long ago that I recall this fresh-faced lad running up and down the green near my home helping old ladies with their shopping bags. He was always ready to do a good turn for anyone in need and you only need to ask around the town for examples of his kindness and generosity. Whenever he is in the area he can be found opening fêtes and helping charities, donating signed footballs, and so on. Where this misguided person has got his information from I just fail to understand. Anyway, carry on with the good work, Emlyn. We still love you in Barrow. Signed: Old Age Pensioner.'

In many ways I was lucky to have the most marvellous and understanding parents. Perhaps it was fortunate for us all that I was not at home during those teenage years when children and parents often come into conflict over the hours and the company they keep. I was still a boy when I left home for Blackpool and I was so keen to be a footballer that I used to make a habit of not drinking or smoking. And I always liked to be in bed early.

Whenever I went home to Barrow in those early days I used to be so pleased to be with them that I rarely went out.

Then, thirteen years ago, I met Barbara and my life changed. After having such a wonderful mother I was doubly lucky in meeting the girl who became the ideal wife. It was an odd meeting, in a way typical of my habit of getting things wrong at first. I was in the Dreadnought Bar in Barrow, a bar named after the nuclear submarine which had been built over the bridge at Vickers-Armstrong. I had just joined Liverpool and was out for a drink with some of my friends. I saw a girl I knew and sat with her. In the company was another girl. I was intrigued by her. She looked rather thin and I decided that she was attractive, but in a funny sort of way. It was an attractiveness that I could not explain to myself. I left her and extended the arm of chivalry to the girl I knew and walked her home. But all the way I was questioning her about the thin girl.

I was told she was called Barbara Dixon, hailed from Carlisle and did a lot of work for the local youth theatre. In fact she had appeared on Border Television as a singer. My interest was growing. Two weeks later I returned to the Dreadnought Bar and the two girls were there again. I bought them a drink, and sat between them. As usual the place was packed and it could take up to twenty minutes to be served at the bar. I finished my Coca Cola, but I was reluctant to go to the bar. I might lose my place next to the thin girl in whom I now had a firm interest. I sat and talked and saw that she had an untouched Babycham alongside the one she was drinking. Cheekily, perhaps, I poured it and started to sip at it. Then the awful truth dawned. It had been bought for her by another lad and he had watched me pour it for myself and start to drink it. When we got up to move elsewhere he decided to react. An argument developed and Barbara said: 'Come on, let's get out of here before there is real trouble.'

As one who had recently signed for Liverpool, that kind of trouble was something I could do without. We left together, and only football trips have separated us ever since.

At one stage during our courtship it looked as though the Dixon family would be moving back to Carlisle. Her

father worked for British Rail and there was talk of a transfer in the air. Fortunately it did not materialize, and soon
I was adding a wedding-ring to the engagement-ring I
bought on the trip to Mexico for the 1970 World Cup.

Nerves jangled on my wedding-day. I never realized the
sense of occasion that prevails when the bells are ringing.
It was a glorious summer's day on Walney Island, where
Barbara lived. I arrived early with my father and David and,
almost inevitably I suppose, they suggested we walk to the
nearby King Alfred Hotel for a steadying pint. My mother
was furious. I recall her shouting after my father: 'Don't
you dare come into the church smelling of beer. I will never
forgive the three of you if you do.' They had a couple of
pints of bitter each, I had a glass of lager. It was a funny
scene. They flanked me like a pair of bouncers and I think
they must have been able to sense the anxiety that was
within me. Suddenly, almost together they said: 'Come on,
let's jump into the car and start driving. Let's just drive
as far as we can.' I could not see the funny side of that.
We strolled down to the church. Mother was frowning, but
soon all was forgotten.

Barbara looked beautiful in church. I don't think she has
ever looked better except, perhaps, during the time she was
pregnant with Emma.

The birth of our daughter was an unforgettable experience. It was the most momentous thing that had ever happened to me. Throughout the pregnancy my father had kept
saying to me, 'Think boy, think boy.' David's wife had had
three girls and there was a danger that there would not be
a young male Hughes to carry on the family name. All our
hearts were set on a little boy and eventually Barbara's time
came. We were at home, early in the evening, when she
announced in a very matter-of-fact way that I ought to be
taking her to hospital. Baby, she said, was on his way.

Suddenly I felt inadequate. I was lost. My parents were away on holiday. My only duty was to drive Barbara to the maternity hospital in Southport, but I had to have a shoulder to lean on. I just didn't know what to do. I thought of John Toshack's wife, Sue, and telephoned her asking for help. What she was supposed to do in the way of assistance I have no idea. Anyway she offered to ride to the hospital with us. When we arrived Barbara went away with a couple of nurses and Sue and I were left in a small room. Soon afterwards a nurse came to me and said: 'You might as well go home because nothing will happen for a couple of hours.'

If she had said ten hours there was no way that I would leave that hospital. I just sat and twitched and Sue stayed with me as we waited for news. It was to be a Caesarean birth.

Nurses were going back and forth. Women on trolleys were being pushed in and out of doors. Babies were crying in the distance. I felt so helpless and nervous as the hours went by. All those old pictures of the worried father-to-be anxiously pacing the floor waiting for news became a reality. We were told that Barbara was going into the theatre and we could see the door. My eyes never left it. A nurse came out carrying what looked like a bundle. I said to Sue, 'That's the baby,' and as the nurse walked past she winked at me. It's a boy, I thought, she has winked at me to let me know.

Silly thoughts, I know because the nurse was not to know that I was wishing for a male heir. She called that she was taking the baby to be cleaned up and that she would be back soon. The nurse returned and handed me the baby. I looked down and, honestly, it was like looking in a mirror. Sue just peeked and gasped, 'It's you.'

It was a girl, too, but who cared about that now? The

little round face was a treasure. It was soft and beautiful with none of the crinkled skin look that goes with babies born naturally. I was as proud as Punch. My daughter. My little girl. My Emma.

I was the proudest father in the world from that moment. When Barbara and Emma came home I used to take the baby everywhere. At around the time she was just starting to walk – a proper little madam who was into everything – we took her on holiday to the Spanish island of Ibiza. The other residents at the hotel made me the butt of their standing joke. They dubbed me the 'Dad of the Year' because everywhere that I went, Emma went too. If she was not sleeping she was with me. If I went for a walk or a drink or merely lazed on the beach, we were inseparable.

A couple of years ago, in her first year at infants school, I went with her to their own little sports day. Only one event existed for the babies of the school – the egg-and-spoon race. It was a thirty-yard meander with a tennis ball precariously balanced on a dessert spoon. Looking back now, I am amazed that I was desperately hoping she would win. It was almost a throwback to the days when I was competing in school sports and my father was always at the side encouraging me. Before she went to school, at five and a half years old, I was instilling in her the need to win. I said that it was important for her and for me. Barbara had to stop me. 'For goodness' sake, Emlyn, you are talking about a little girl in an egg-and-spoon race with an infants' class. She is not about to play in the European Cup final.'

Off we went to the sports meeting and we were there as close to the finish as we could get. They set off and Emma was going well with two-thirds of the distance covered. She was in the lead. I could not resist cheering her on. 'Go on, Emma, love,' I shouted.

She heard my voice and stopped to give me a wave. The opposition flashed past and she could only finish third. I resolved to do something about her competitive spirit.

The old Hughes attitude soon showed itself. The following year Emma was back at the starting line for the egg-and-spoon race and the fifty-yard dash. I was at Wolverhampton and telephoned her from the hotel where I was staying. The pep talk was reminiscent of the previous year only this time I threw in the incentive of a nice present. She won both races and when I arrived home there were two sheets of yellow paper with a gold disc in the centre. These were her winners' certificates; her pride and joy. They now rank in importance in the Hughes household at Formby, Lancashire, over anything I have ever done.

Forget that terrific picture of my holding the European Cup aloft. Forget those groups of legendary Liverpool football teams. The gold disc on yellow paper is the prize that counts.

Emlyn junior is the character of the house. A little tearaway who is as sharp as a needle with his wit. I hope I am not overdoing the proud father routine again, but there are moments when his natural gifts for playing with a ball actually stagger me. I have never imagined that a youngster could display so much ability when still short of his fourth birthday.

Already he is a sports nut. Whatever sport appears on television it seems that he knows the personalities. He can recite the names of the full line-ups of Liverpool, Everton, Wolves, Manchester United, Manchester City and several other teams.

At the moment he is crazy about goalkeepers. Paul Bradshaw, the Wolves' goalkeeper, is his hero. I am sure that whenever he comes along to watch us play he never looks at any other member of the team. I have a little ritual at

the end of games. I know where the family sit. If we have
won Barbara gives me a gentle 'well done' signal, Emma
sits all coy and demure because already she believes she
is a young lady and that is how little women behave.
Not Emlyn, however. He is usually up on his feet punch-
ing the air with both arms. That is how they all reacted
when we went to Manchester City early in the 1979–80
season.

We won 3–2, and after showering and changing I went
along to the players' lounge where friend and foe drink
together and wives and friends join in. As I walked through
the door the people were all having a good laugh about
something. Second nature made me sense that young Emlyn
was involved in some way. Barbara said to me straight
away, 'What on earth are we going to do with your son?'

Whenever he is in any kind of trouble it is always 'your
son', as if I am solely responsible for his breeding, behaviour
and development. Then I heard the story.

It transpired that as Joe Corrigan, the giant Manchester
City goalkeeper, walked into the room and moved towards
the bar to join a friend, Emlyn decided to act. He moved
up to Joe, tapped his leg and as Joe looked down from his
6 ft 5 ins as though there was a small dog rubbing against
him he saw my young one looking up, winking and saying
in a very old-fashioned way: 'Bad luck, Joe.' Everyone saw
him. Everyone heard him.

Early in 1980 Wolves played Everton at Molineux. It was
a wild, wet and muddy day; the sort of occasion only the
devil could have inflicted upon the football race. The game
was abysmal. It was o–o at the end and if we had played
for a fortnight I am sure that is how the score would have
stayed. For long, barren periods of midfield deadlock Paul
Bradshaw – the lad's unquestioned hero – was walking and
jogging along the edge of his penalty area just trying to keep

warm. Emlyn watched every move he made and finally he turned to Barbara and said, 'Doesn't Paul look sad?'

After the match there was again laughter in the air as I entered the lounge and Paul came up to me.

'What about your lad?'

'All right, what has he done this time?'

Paul reported: 'I was at the bar ordering a drink when he wrapped his arms round both my legs and said, "I am just giving you a love because you looked so sad out there."'

The sad aspect of all the delights and pleasure that young Emlyn brings us is that my father died during the period when Barbara was pregnant. He, and his 'think boys' theory, wanted a grandson so desperately that when the baby arrived and father had passed on the event seemed something of an anti-climax.

Of course, Emlyn is a little gem. He could write his name at three years of age and while this does not make him a prodigy there is something in his mental approach that shows him to be a very quick-witted youngster. Emma is different. She is prepared to plod along, working hard and sorting things out for herself whereas he is a kid who finds things easy. He is my best pal. His little beaming face is a pick-me-up whenever I get home. He always has something to tell me; there is constantly something that he thinks we should sort out together. Just looking at him sometimes makes me laugh.

Whenever I see footballers going off the rails – and there have been a few – I thank God for the solid reliability of my family life. When I think of my mother, and of Barbara, I know that I could not have spent my time with two better women. There has always been great trust and understanding.

When the time came for me to leave Liverpool I could

have chosen my club: Manchester City, Wolves, Southampton, Bristol City were among those who wanted me as a player. From the Third and Fourth Divisions there were offers inviting me to become a player-manager. I knew that whatever decision I arrived at, Barbara would go along with me. There was no need to burden her with a share of the decision-making. She has always accepted that I must be the master of my own destiny. And I certainly would not try to tell her what kind of meat to buy at the butchers.

Barbara's strength is her straightness. She is a matter-of-fact girl and I know that I could never have married anyone whose head could be turned by whatever modest success might have come my way.

There is another lady, too, to whom I feel I owe something of a debt: Minnie Firth, who looked after me as warmly as she would one of her own family during the time I lodged with her in Liverpool before my marriage.

Mrs Firth deserves only the best and I have told her more than once that if anyone ever causes her any trouble then she has only to let me know. We have remained firm friends and I often take the children to see her. She tells Barbara that I was always her favourite lodger. With her kind of hospitality and understanding still warmly secure in my memory I can say the feeling is mutual.

16

Ask Me
Another

WHEREVER I GO THERE ARE ALWAYS PEOPLE asking me to settle their private arguments. Who scored the goals in the 1974 Cup final? Who was the last player to notch a hat-trick for England?

Footballers are just as bad when they are together. We always fall for the catch question. For instance, 'Who played for Manchester City one Saturday and Manchester United the following week, and not a ha'penny changed hands?'

They think, and rack their brains and throw in a few names and finally give in.

Answer: Beswick Silver Prize Band!

I have never considered myself an expert on these

matters, but being a team captain along with the Welsh rugby union international Gareth Edwards on the BBC television sports quiz programme 'A Question of Sport' has made me a special victim for the catch question.

Actually I love the programme. I first went on it as a guest, at the invitation of the producer Hazel Lewthwaite, when Cliff Morgan and Henry Cooper were the captains. It was then that I realized what a bundle of laughs the programme could be. Amazingly, Henry, who was one of the greatest and most popular boxers this country has ever produced, had an uncanny knack of failing whenever the question centred around his own sport. There was one classic occasion when two black heavyweights in a championship fight were briefly shown on the film. Henry had to identify the winner of the fight, for one of them was truly poleaxed.

Henry was rubbing his chin and thinking deeply. 'I should know 'im,' he kept saying in that familiar Cockney accent. As it happened I recognized them as Ernie Terrell and Zora Folley. A glorious punch from Terrell ended it.

Henry was puzzling away and suddenly, with the assistance of my team captain Cliff, I set up Britain's great heavyweight for a fall.

'I should know 'im,' Henry was saying and I turned to Cliff and said with my hand over my mouth, but just loud enough so that Henry would hear: 'It's Folley.' Cliff carried on the charade with a loud 'Hush'.

Suddenly Henry dived in: 'I know. It's Zora Folley.'

'Wrong,' said the question-master David Vine. We chipped in with Ernie Terrell for the bonus point and fell about laughing.

Cliff was terrific fun, and a brilliant after-dinner speaker. He spoke at a couple of my testimonial year functions. He talks with feeling, with a pride of his native Welsh valleys that can bring a lump to the hardest man's throat even in the build-up to a funny story. He is at his best when talking about those Welsh rugby union giants who emerged from desperately poor backgrounds to become lions in the game.

He has shot up the television ladder and when it was decided to re-vamp the quiz he invited Gareth and myself to be the new captains, with David Coleman as questionmaster. He said they wanted people whom the younger viewers could identify as current stars.

Perhaps we have brought more of a laugh to the proceedings. It has moved from being a fairly serious quiz to all-round entertainment, although sometimes our guests have given us bigger laughs than we ever anticipated.

Tony Currie, that incredibly gifted midfield player, provided one outrageous moment. He was asked to identify an occasion. We peered into the small monitor and he was asked to name the teams taking part in a football match.

One team were in green, the other in blue. It was a huge Continental stadium and I recognized Bertie Vogts, Gerd Mueller and one or two other West Germans in their change strip of green. From England's tour of Eastern Europe in 1974 I recognized several East German players in blue. It was obvious that this was the classic, historical confrontation between the two Germanys in the 1974 World Cup.

I looked at Tony. He said: 'Got it. No problem.'

'Go on then,' I said.

He said slowly: 'Er ... it's Norwich City v. Ipswich Town.' More falling about by the rest of us.

The British boxer Maurice Hope showed – as we all have from time to time – that none of us are ready to challenge for Magnus Magnusson's 'Mastermind' series. Maurice was shown a film of two black boxers and asked to identify one of them.

He fell silent. Ten seconds of silence on television can seem like an age. David Coleman asked him if he understood the question. He nodded that he did and so, once again, David broke the marathon silence to ask him to identify one of the fighters.

'One of the black ones?' queried Maurice.

Part of the delight of being on the programme is being able to meet such marvellous personalities from other sports. Gareth, of course, is a legend and his half-back partnership with Barry John ranks as one of the greatest half-back pairings that rugby union has ever known. Their understanding behind the rampaging Welsh pack was legendary. To hear John Toshack, another Welshman, talking about them, was to wonder at the reverence that crept into his voice.

Gareth knew that I used to feed on his stories and I recall telling him that I proposed to ring Barry at his home at six o'clock one Sunday evening. Barry had been well primed, because as he picked up the telephone he announced: 'This is the King speaking.' He was known as 'King Barry' by Welsh rugby followers. Who, in Wales, is not a rugby follower?

I have met Barry on several occasions and it says something of the spirit of the Welsh and their brightness on the field when I relate an incident they often talk about. A ball is booted upfield into Welsh territory and the moment it leaves the kicker's foot Barry has made up his mind. He says to himself: I am too valuable to get under this to be buried by a pack of forwards.

So he shouts: 'J.P.R.' And J.P.R. Williams, a brilliant full-back, would gallop up to do the dirty work with all the bravery in the world.

Gareth and Barry say they had such a fine understanding that one of their unfulfilled ambitions was to make a unique combination at a dropped goal. Gareth was to drop the ball for Barry's kick.

Gareth told me: 'I am not sure how that would figure within the laws of the game. And, anyway, we would need to be playing England to be so many points ahead that it would not matter.'

These are the stories we used to tell to get the audience warmed up before the start of the quiz which was filmed in Manchester on Sunday afternoons.

I have had some incredible publicity and recognition through the show. Old ladies and non-footballing people stop me in the street and say: 'Great, Emlyn. Marvellous last night.' Then I realized that they were not talking about my ability as a footballer, but by the entertainment they could derive from 'A Question of Sport'.

People write complaining about a bias towards certain sports – too many northern footballers, not enough southern croquet-players, and so on. I get blamed for all sorts of things but, in fact, the guests are chosen by the BBC and I never have any idea who is likely to be on my team.

I receive letters like: 'Why don't you look around and invite so-and-so, the unbelievably brilliant one-eyed shinty player from the Outer Hebrides? He has been ten years at the top without recognition.'

The rewards, however, do not come from the recognition, although it is very pleasant. The greatest moment that Gareth and I experienced came towards the end of the last series. Hazel Lewthwaite came into the room with a smile spread across her face. The programme, she announced, had just broken through the magical ten-million barrier according to the JicTar ratings.

We knew that television people live and die by the viewing figures and this, for Hazel, was gold medal land. To know that we had played some small part in the success of the programme was rewarding enough. We were invited, almost immediately, to be the team captains in the next series.

Cliff Morgan and Hazel Lewthwaite have always said that they find me good television interview material. I can face dodgy questions and treat them squarely without tumbling headlong into controversy. I try to smile about most things. Cheerfulness comes easily to me.

It would be nice to think that I might have some small future to play on the box in the corner of most people's living-rooms.

17

The Future

WHAT LIES AHEAD? WHATEVER HAPPENS NO ONE can take away the fact that I have played around eight hundred games of first-class football. With Blackpool, Liverpool, Wolves and the England full and Under-23 teams it has been a career beyond my wildest expectations. When I used to sit and wonder in those Blackpool digs so many years ago I never imagined that I would enjoy so much fun and success.

Hopefully there will be many more games to come for Wolves. The only doubts concerns the old legs that have taken such a pounding over the years. For fourteen years, during all those seasons when Liverpool were competing for every trophy that was on offer, I rarely missed a match. I was playing more than sixty games in some seasons and there always seemed to be club or England tours abroad. I was fortunate to escape major injury but slowly, remorselessly, all the activity was taking a toll on my knees. First it was the right one, then the left, which is puffed with fluid as I move towards the end of this book.

The first hint of trouble came in the 1978–9 season. We were playing at home against Spurs. I turned round quickly to chase a ball back to Ray Clemence with the Spurs Argentinian player Ricardo Villa running alongside. When I saw that Clemence was sure to collect the ball safely I stopped dead in my tracks by digging my toes into the turf. Instantly I felt something go under my knee-cap. I was in agony. I had to leave the field. I missed the next match because the pain and swelling was slow to subside and the club sent me to see a specialist. The problem was certainly not cartilage, nor were the ligaments damaged. It was a mystery. And after three weeks things were no better. I had to slide myself gently sideways out of my car by holding on to the top of the door-frame. Then I had to massage the knee myself before I could even begin to limp along. If anything it was getting worse and, full of worries, I had a second appointment with the specialist.

He decided to make X-ray examinations of both knees so that he could compare the good to the bad and the ugly. It all revealed that the gristle between my knee-caps and my knee-bone, which allows the joint to swing easily, had simply been worn away by so many seasons of twisting and turning and running. The two were now rubbing together, which was causing all the pain, inflammation and fluid. He advised me to keep my thigh muscles tight with exercise and that with regular walking the bones would form their own groove and eventually I would have complete freedom of movement again. Rest and exercise did the trick and now the right knee is trouble-free.

I had just settled in at Wolves when the left knee began to play up with the same trouble. It wasn't bad enough to keep me out of the team, but I was unable to train as I would have liked in the autumn of 1979.

If, like my right knee, it clears up completely then everything will be fine. I will carry on playing, but I must be constantly on my guard against causing permanent damage.

When I was out of action at Liverpool it seemed I could not open a newspaper without reading some conjecture about my future. Everybody wanted to have a guess. In fact, six very good clubs telephoned me to say that if I felt like trying something else they would offer me a good contract as player-manager.

They were not rubbish clubs without hope. Everyone had potential and I was flattered. Two were from the Second Division, three from the Third and one from the Fourth. All were from areas where crowds would respond to any success. All the offers were tempting and while my Liverpool future did not look too bright – Alan Hansen was playing well alongside Phil Thompson, and Alan Kennedy had settled in at left-back – there were other things on my mind. The home international championships and the England summer tour to Bulgaria, Sweden and Austria were due to take place and I felt I would be able to gauge my future better afterwards.

I promised them all I would let them know how I felt when I returned from the tour. I enjoyed it. I played one of my best ever games for England against Sweden and that, more than anything, convinced me that I still had a place in the First Division.

Ron Greenwood gave me even greater encouragement. He knew my future was regarded as uncertain by some people. He may even have felt that I was no longer his No. 1 choice at centre-back, because Dave Watson and Phil Thompson had looked happy together.

Anyway, Greenwood took me to one side during the tour and said, 'I want you in my plans all the way through to the European Championship finals in Rome, and if you're still playing after that then I will want you through until the World Cup in Spain in 1982. But I want you to be fair with me and understand that I can hardly pick you if you're in the reserves every week.'

Of course I had to agree with him. I have every faith in Ron Greenwood and agreed that he could only do what he honestly believed to be the right thing for England.

When I arrived home I spoke to two other men whose judgement I respect and admire. I knew that from Bill Shankly and Joe Mercer I would get straight to the point. I knew that if they thought I was wasting my time chasing further England caps and First Division honours they would be the first people to tell me. Both of them urged me to carry on playing as long as I could, to get as much enjoyment from the game as possible. They were old professionals and remembered how badly they had missed the playing side once they had retired. They had wanted to return, but there was no way.

I knew what they were talking about. There is a special camaraderie about a football team's dressing-room. The humour is rich and ripe. There are some razor-sharp wits about and nine out of ten footballers gear their lives to a laugh. But there is more to it than that. It's a life of ups and downs. It's precarious . . . and that is part of the undeniable appeal of the game.

There is the long marathon of an English season. The kick-off is always full of promise. The grass is fresh, and so are the players and the fans. Autumn brings a settling-down period. Then there are the cold, dark depths of mid-winter where the teams with strength and character and skill establish themselves in the leading positions, ready for the run-down into spring and the share-out of the trophies.

All that is something that Shanks and Joe Mercer convinced me I should not give up. I put forward no argument against the idea. I briefly entertained the thought of going into a lower division as player-manager – but only briefly – and dismissed that notion when it was pretty obvious that at my age it was a roundabout way of trying to get back into the First Division.

I now know I made the right decision in joining John Barnwell and Richie Barker at Wolves. I still enjoy playing. I love working for them. No matter what anyone says about my play, as long as my employers are happy with me I will continue on as a player.

One thing is certain: I will not be leaving Molineux of my own accord to join another club. I am with Wolves for as long as they want me and when the time comes for me to leave I hope it will be to join some other team as player-manager or manager. I have had a marvellous run and Wolves are great for me. They are a club with ambitions. The ground is splendid and there are plans to make it the most modern stadium in the Football League. If I can help them towards having the right team to go with it then I will have done my job.

When Wolves brought me down from Liverpool in the summer of 1979 they offered me a three-year contract. They allowed me to live in a hotel – I am still there between spells at home with my family in Formby – and paid me excellent wages. I was aware that knee trouble could flare up at any time and, because I like to think I have never cheated anyone, I declined the three-year terms.

I said I would sign if they insisted but, in all honesty, I did not think my legs would last that long. I said I would hate to find myself in the position where I had to pack up after eighteen months, leaving them to pay off the remainder of the contract. I suggested that I sign for two years and then, if I were still going strong and they were happy with me, I would take on another year without any demands from me for extra wages or a signing-on fee. We agreed on that.

Now, thanks to John and Richie, I'm having a remarkable apprenticeship in club management. I am making no criticism of Bob Paisley or Joe Fagan, who have plenty on their plates at Anfield, but I have learned an incredible amount from the Wolves pair who, after all, are much closer to my age-group.

John has been fantastic with me. He has told me of the things that go on at football clubs, of the boardroom dealings and conduct. He knows that when I leave Molineux it will be to take over some other club and he is preparing me for that day.

I know now that if I had gone from Liverpool straight into management I would have been out on my backside within six months. I would not have known where to start. John has told me things I never even knew went on. He has to haggle over players' contracts, organize scouting systems, deal with players' domestic problems, talk to directors about possible new signings ... I used to be under the impression that a manager picked a team and then went out to watch them play. It's far from that!

My rôle at Wolves is as captain. I'm John's liaison officer on and off the field. Together we are working hard in the hope that we can give the Wolves supporters the brand-new tomorrow so many of them are always dreaming about. The old ones love to yarn about the good old days of Stan Cullis's teams. We want to give them something new to talk about.

To do that we all know that we have to work extra hard. We all know that we are not in Liverpool's class and no one at Molineux has ever suggested that we are. We are not filled with talented internationals like Ray Clemence, Kenny Dalglish or Phil Thompson, but those rewards will come if we keep grafting. We cannot turn on the tap the way they can, but it is coming ...

Whatever a man does in life he should always be striving for improvement. When I drove down to Wolves on my first day I knew that I could help the club up the First Division table. I was not the only new figure at Molineux. Barnwell and Barker had not been there long. I was followed by Andy Gray and Dave Thomas and we are all in the business of putting Wolves back at the top. If we succeed then the mission will have been accomplished.

Then I will be able to leave the First Division a happy man. I will be looking for another challenge. I know it will be hard. I have heard enough stories from John Toshack, who had it rough when he first took over at Swansea.

Everything will fall on my shoulders. But I know also that for a manager to succeed he must be part of a trio who are prepared to work together, as solid as a rock, without ever getting in each other's way. That has always been a part of Liverpool's secret and, make no mistake, football takes its standards from Anfield.

When I move into management I should have the right qualifications: played all over the world, won all the medals, studied under the best.

Epilogue

I THOUGHT I HAD FINISHED WRITING THIS BOOK. My notes were put away. All the words were safely gathered in and I picked up the telephone to speak to Bill Shankly. I wanted to tell him what I had done. Bill's views are consistently a dialogue of wisdom and confidence.

I told him I had set out to play the game. I wanted to pen a fair reflection on my life, to draw a few laughs, recall some of the good times and avoid, if possible, plunging into controversy and criticism of people in the game that has given me such a rewarding life.

That is the pitfall many players fall into. Sad to say, it's the goal of many. But football and footballers take too many knocks. I have had some wonderful times and even in those early dark days at Liverpool, when I felt the welcome was not instantly warm, I could understand the feelings of the established players. I felt, if only for Emlyn junior, that I wanted a book he could pick up in years to come and read about my life and times in the game.

It has become apparent throughout the weeks of making recollections and putting them down on paper that I have drawn heavily on the inspiration of two men in particular – my father and Shanks.

It was Shanks who once said of himself: 'When I die I only hope that people will be able to say he played the game, he was fair, he never cheated anyone. And if they can say that I know I will be able to rest in peace.'

I would like to think that I, too, have followed those guidelines.

In my telephone call I explained to Bill that I had tried to get away from the usual kick-by-kick formula of so many football books.

I said to him: 'To tell you the truth, Bill, the whole fabric is woven around three men. Myself, of course, my father, and you.'

There was a long silence at the other end. I sensed he was winding himself up to tell me I had got things wrong. Suddenly the old, familiar Rob Roy voice exploded down the line.

'Hell's bells, son. If that's so you have created a best-seller.'

The last word simply had to come from the old commander who has backed me from the day I first met him. What a trooper.